Published in the UK in 2023
by Icon Books Ltd, Omnibus Business Centre,
39–41 North Road, London N7 9DP
info@iconbooks.com
www.iconbooks.com

Sold in the UK, Europe and Asia by
Faber & Faber Ltd, Bloomsbury House,
74–77 Great Russell Street,
London WC1B 3DA or their agents

Distributed in the UK, Europe and Asia
by Grantham Book Services, Trent Road,
Grantham NG31 7XQ

Distributed in Australia and New Zealand
by Allen & Unwin Pty Ltd, PO Box 8500,
83 Alexander Street, Crows Nest, NSW 2065

Distributed in South Africa
by Jonathan Ball, Office B4, The District,
41 Sir Lowry Road, Woodstock 7925

Distributed in India by Penguin Books India,
7th Floor, Infinity Tower-C, DLF Cyber City,
Gurgaon 122002, Haryana

Publisher: Jason Hook
Commissioning editor: Kate Duffy
Designer: Luke Herriott
Illustrator: Robert Brandt

ISBN: 978-1-78578-943-4

Printed in China

10 9 8 7 6 5 4 3 2 1

PSYCHOLOGY

Consultant Editor
DR JENNIFER WILD

ICON BOOKS

1 COGNITIVE PSYCHOLOGY   8

2 SOCIAL PSYCHOLOGY   28

3 LEARNING   48

4 BIOLOGICAL PSYCHOLOGY   68

INTRODU

Psychology reaches every conceivable area of our development, from how we form bonds as babies to how we think and interact with the world. Psychological findings have a direct impact on how we lead our lives. Understand psychology and you understand what it is to be human. But which findings and theories are the most relevant to us? And what exactly do they all mean? We need a short cut, and this book will provide just that, guiding you to understand how psychology helps humanity evolve when applied to some of society's most complex issues.

The journey begins with cognitive psychology, revealing the processes that enable us to see, think and decide. We uncover uncomfortable truths about how memory works and why we're unreliable witnesses. This leads on to the power of groups and investigations belonging to the realm of social psychology. Why and how do groups sway our thinking with, at times, significant consequences? We learn about how we learn, how the brain makes a memory and why false memories are easily experienced. We discover what happens when things go wrong with disorders such as synaesthesia, where the brain blends senses, and facial blindness, when people are unable to recognise others.

The book then leads into our biology, where there's opportunity to become senseless about our senses –

‚ION

there are over fifty! We learn what is just the right amount of stress to peak our performance, and discern how psychologists measure stress. We also see what happens in the brain when we take drugs, from antidepressants to marijuana. We dabble in child's play, and walk through our early years to discover how our family bonds shape our strategies for coping many years later.

Then we zoom in on what makes us individuals, what separates the good from the great, what motivates us. We turn to intelligence – the many types, and the ones linked to strong leaders. We uncover the theories of how we construct reality. We see how psychology applies science to mental health to develop treatments that work. We grasp how cognitive behavioural therapy – one of the most effective treatments for depression and anxiety disorders – guides patients to become scientists, testing and updating their thoughts with experiments in an approach that leads to lasting cures. Finally, our journey ends on a high, tapping in to positive psychology to uncover the ingredients for happy living, how to train a happy mind and how to flourish.

In short, this book navigates human growth, delving into some of the most revolutionary contributions psychology has made to our knowledge of how our minds evolve throughout our lives.

Enjoy the journey!

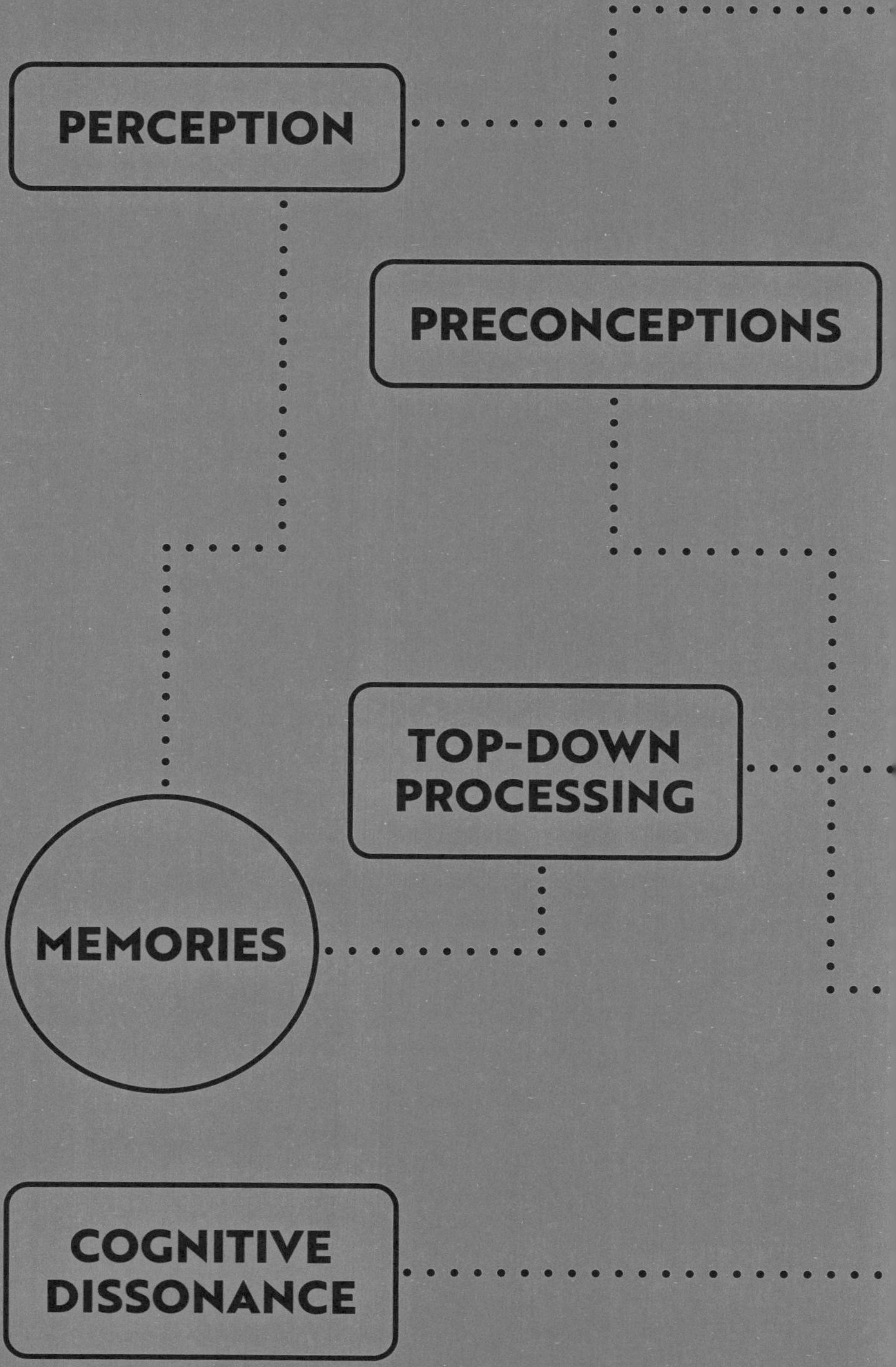
PERCEPTION
PRECONCEPTIONS
TOP-DOWN PROCESSING
MEMORIES
COGNITIVE DISSONANCE

CHAPTER 1

COGNITIVE PSYCHOLOGY

EXPECTATIONS

GROUPTHINK

BIAS

INTRODUCTION

How do we experience our lives? Psychologists say this is down to how we perceive the world, make our memories and decisions, and how we think. In this chapter we discover all about the processes that allow us to make sense of what we encounter.

Every waking minute, we are bombarded with sensory information. To make sense of it all, the brain works at 120 metres per second, testing **HYPOTHESES** and updating conclusions as more information reaches the eye. This process is called **TOP-DOWN PROCESSING**, where we use what we already know to interpret new information. It means we see what we expect to see. **GIBSON'S ECOLOGICAL THEORY**, however, suggests it is **BOTTOM-UP PROCESSING** that rules the roost, with information originating in the environment, travelling to the eye and then the brain. According to this theory, we must perceive the world in order to survive it, and we do this from the moment we are born.

Our memories play an important part in how we perceive the world. But how reliable are they? By studying inconsistencies in how people remembered major events, Neisser observed that our memories change over time. Nader and LeDoux's work seems to suggest that every time we remember an event, we rewrite it, and it's the rewritten version we remember the next time. According to **RECONSOLIDATION THEORY**, when we recall an event, the memory trace in the brain becomes plastic and must be consolidated all over again or it will be wiped out. Our memories are fragile.

Loftus found that any number of things can change a memory, such as our expectations, biases and even language. Using a dramatic word such as 'crashed' when questioning an eyewitness to a road traffic accident could give rise to a memory of cars travelling at faster speeds than when dry language is used, such as asking about how two vehicles 'collided'. For this reason, eyewitness testimony is unreliable, and it's also possible to create **FALSE MEMORIES** through the power of suggestion.

Theories of how memories are stored should help to explain how they are recalled, but there is debate about this process, too. Memory was seen initially as short or long term. However, Baddeley updated this concept, positing working memory as capable of storing as well as processing information in the short term. In 1972, Craik and Lockhart proposed the processing model of memory, which sees a link between depth of processing and how long memories last.

Turning to how we think, it was Janis who discovered how easily groups sway our views. In a group, we're more likely to dismiss alternative perspectives, as it's easier to blend in than speak up and stand out. Pressure influences our thinking and decision making. Under stress, the brain will take short cuts, using our intuition rather than deliberate and logical thinking. Although risky, sometimes it is the short cut that is the best cut.

COGNITIVE PSYCHOLOGY MAP

METHOD

HYPOTHESES
Predictions based on what we think might happen.

UNCONSCIOUS INFERENCES
Influence of memory and experience on perception, both of which unite with incoming stimuli to create a full picture (Helmholtz).

GIBSON'S ECOLOGICAL THEORY
Information originates in the environment; we must perceive the world to survive it, and we do this from birth.

PERCEPTION
Active process that involves memory and experience, rather than just the passive acceptance of incoming stimuli (Helmholtz).

TOP-DOWN PROCESSING
Using what we already know to interpret new information; we see what we expect to see (Gregory).

SCHEMA
Mental representation of our experiences, based on prior experience and memory.

ILLUSION

AFFORDANCE
Opportunity for action provided by the environment, which gives meaning, i.e. a bike affords an opportunity to travel (Gibson).

ATKINSON AND SHIFFRIN'S MULTI-STORE MODEL
Existence of three memory stores: 1) sensory memory; 2) short-term memory; 3) long-term memory. Information is transferred between the three compartments in order.

RECONSOLIDATION THEORY
Every time something is remembered we rewrite our memory. Long-term memories need to be reconsolidated when recalled or they're wiped out (Nader and LeDoux).

BOTTOM-UP PROCESSING
Perception occurs bottom-up, from the environment, to the eye, to the brain (Gibson).

MISINFORMATION EFFECT
Contamination of an existing memory through misleading information after the event, i.e. a witness's memory being altered by inaccurate questioning.

FALSE MEMORIES
'Memories' that have been suggested to us, and that can seem very real, but which are not (Loftus).

COGNITIVE DISSONANCE
Holding two conflicting views at once, causing a misalignment in behaviour and beliefs, and consequently psychological stress (Festinger).

GROUPTHINK
Individual opinions become drowned out by a collective consensus because it's easier to stay quiet than speak up, which can lead to bad outcomes (Janis).

PERCEPTUAL CYCLE
Our experiences of the world are shaped by the interplay of schema and environmental cues; external cues feed back to influence internal schema (Neisser).

Is perception just an experiment?

→ Maybe. When they perform experiments, scientists test hypotheses, which are predictions about what they think might happen. The brain seems to work in the same way, testing hypotheses then using the results to build a picture of what we see.

Our eyes receive visual input, our ears detect sound and our noses sometimes crinkle in response to odours. For decades, psychologists have debated how these sensory signals translate into perceptual experience. How, for example, do we recognise a blurry, furry, stick-chasing object as a dog, or equate a collection of odour molecules to the scent of a rose?

In 1867, German scientist Hermann von Helmholtz described the importance of unconscious inferences. Perception, he realised, is not just the passive acceptance of incoming stimuli, but an active process that involves memory and experience.

Building on this idea, in 1970, British psychologist Richard Gregory proposed that we actively construct our perception of reality. He argued that our senses are bombarded with signals that are frequently ambiguous and difficult to interpret. To make sense of them, we rely heavily on information that is already stored in the brain. We create

hypotheses of what we are experiencing, based on prior knowledge and past experiences. The brain essentially guesses what it is seeing, and then updates working hypotheses as more information reaches the eye. According to his model, perception is a form of top-down processing, where we use what we already know to interpret new information.

Gregory argued that certain visual illusions, such as the Necker cube and the hollow-face illusion, demonstrate the top-down processing of perceptual information. For example, when a 3D mask of Charlie Chaplin's face is slowly rotated, there comes a point where the concave back of the mask 'pops out' to show a fully formed convex face that is moving in the opposite direction. Our brain expects to see convex faces, which are far more common than concave ones, and so imposes this interpretation upon us. Sometimes we see what we expect to see, rather than what is actually there.

TOP-DOWN PROCESSING

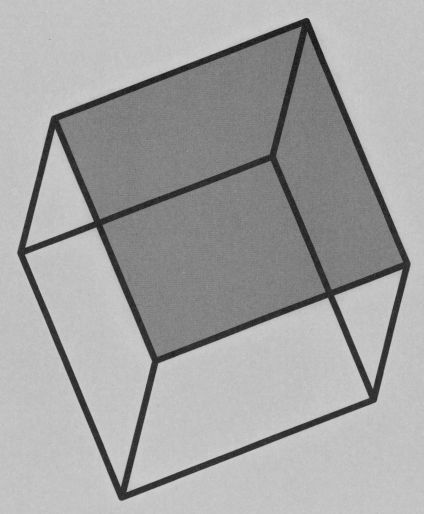

This is the Necker cube. What do you see? Stare at it for a while and the image becomes unstable. The coloured square flicks between back and front, as a single physical pattern generates alternating interpretations. According to Gregory, the conflict occurs because the brain develops two equally plausible hypotheses for what is being seen, and is unable to choose between them. Top-down processing must drive the illusion, because the sensory input remains unchanged throughout.

Is what we see what we get?

→ According to one school of thought, yes, it is! Our visual experience of the world is predominantly shaped by the information that hits our eyes, rather than by any preconceptions that are stored in our brains.

Visual perception is a tricky beast. How are the light particles that hit our retinas converted into perceptions of people, buildings, bicycles and other objects? Does perception occur top-down, with memory and prior knowledge trumping incoming visual stimuli, or does it occur bottom-up, with what we actually see having a major influence on experience? In the 1960s and 1970s, James J. Gibson argued for the latter.

According to Gibson, ordinary, real-world experience provides us with more than enough information to make sense of what we see. There is no need for additional processing or interpretation. As we move around the world, our visual input changes. Objects, for example, are seen from different distances and orientations, providing a wealth of data that directly informs perception. As a result, perception is a combination of a person's environment and their interaction with it. Gibson believed that processing occurs in a direct manner, bottom-up, from

the environment, to the eye, to the brain. What we perceive is what we see, rather than what we think we see, and because of this strong environmental influence, it became known as the ecological theory.

Furthermore, Gibson believed that perception depends on embodied action. When we perceive objects, we see them in terms of the possibilities they offer for us to interact with them. An affordance, as he called it, is an opportunity for action – a kettle for boiling, a bicycle for riding, a biscuit for eating – rather than a representation of the world that is independent of our actions. Meaning, he claimed, is what the environment 'affords' the observer.

According to Gibson's theory, no prior experience or learning is required for perception to occur. Instead, the process is innate. It has been forged through evolution because it offers a substantial survival advantage. In order to effectively respond to the environment, an organism must first be able to perceive it.

BOTTOM-UP PROCESSING

According to Gibson, perception occurs bottom-up, from the environment, to the eye, to the brain. When we see a rose, our brain registers exactly that. The pattern of light reaching the eye creates unambiguous information about the qualities of objects in space, for example, their size and location. As we move around the environment, this information changes, generating the raw fuel that is needed for perception. No prior knowledge or experience is required.

How does the brain make a memory?

→ Memory making is an active process of construction rather than a passive reproduction of the past. As a result, our memories can change over time.

Memories are made in the brain. This much is obvious, but the extent to which they are influenced by external events is a matter of debate. When Ulric Neisser first started thinking about this, over 40 years ago, he realised the importance of environmental influences on cognitive processes. Perception, he argued, is an active process in which our experiences of the world are shaped by the interplay between the ideas and suppositions in our brains – so-called 'schema' – and environmental cues. In other words, top-down and bottom-up processing are important for perception, with external cues feeding back to influence internal schema. This is called the perceptual cycle.

Turning his attention to memory, Neisser realised that psychologists would learn little from artificial laboratory studies of word lists and recall. If the environment is important, as he believed, then memory had to be studied in the real world. In a classic study from 1981, Neisser analysed the testimony of Richard Nixon's former advisor, John Dean, from the Watergate scandal. When details of the testimony were compared against transcripts of recorded conversations he had participated in, differences emerged. For example, Dean tended to dramatise events, exaggerate his role and morph together events from different time points into single 'memories'.

According to Neisser, errors like this are common, and they occur because memories are actively constructed rather than passively replayed. His 1986 study, in the wake of the Challenger space shuttle disaster, arrived at a similar conclusion. The recollections of students three years after the tragedy differed substantially from those recorded the day after the explosion.

Memory, Neisser argued, is not an accurate snapshot of a moment, frozen in time. To recall an event, the mind has to actively reconstruct the past, and this process is inevitably influenced by subsequent experience. As a result, memories frequently become distorted, which can be a serious problem, for example, in the realm of eyewitness testimonies.

MEMORY BUILDING

Neisser proposed that just as a contractor builds a house, so our brains actively construct memories. Suppose five years down the line you asked the same contractor to create a copy of the house but didn't give him the original plans. The reconstruction would be similar but not identical to the original. In the same way, memories of past events have to be constructed, and these too become less accurate with time.

Are you a reliable eyewitness?

⟶ **Probably not. We trust our sight more than any other sense, but the truth is that we are often let down by our brain's interpretation of what we're seeing, and by our memories of people and events.**

Eyewitness accounts can be very persuasive. When a victim confidently identifies their attacker from a selection of mugshots, or a courtroom witness swears that they saw the defendant commit an alleged crime, this carries serious weight with police officers and juries. The problem is that eyewitnesses can in fact be highly unreliable.

American cognitive psychologist Elizabeth Loftus pioneered studies in this field, publishing in 1979 her classic work *Eyewitness Testimony*. As countless subsequent studies have confirmed, all kinds of factors influence what a witness thinks they have seen. These include poor viewing conditions, getting only a glimpse of the perpetrator, stress, and expectations and biases – including racial stereotyping.

Another major problem is that our memories are malleable. Hundreds of studies have found that the very act of being questioned can itself implant new memories in a witness, and alter existing ones. For example, if a witness is asked a question that contains a factual error, this can change their memories of what actually happened. This misinformation effect can tamper with memories of everything from what a perpetrator looks like to the layout of the scene of the crime.

Contamination of a genuine memory is bad enough. But as Loftus and other psychologists have shown, we can even come to harbour fully false memories – 'memories' that have been suggested to us, and that can seem very real, but which are not.

The potential dangers of relying too heavily on eyewitness testimony are huge. A 2011 study in the US concluded that faulty eyewitness testimony was implicated in at least three-quarters of cases where convictions were overturned as a result of new DNA analysis. Mistaken eyewitness evidence has sent people not only to prison for decades, but to Death Row.

All of this means that we should be cautious about trusting the report of any eyewitnesses – including ourselves.

MISINFORMATION EFFECT

'34.0 mph'

'HIT'

'30.8 mph'

'COLLIDED'

'SMASHED'

'40.8 mph'

In an early experiment by Loftus and Palmer, participants watched footage of a traffic accident and then answered questions about the speed of the cars involved. Questions including words such as 'smashed' led to higher speed estimates than words such as 'collided', showing that memory can be manipulated just by changing how a question is phrased.

How are our memories stored?

⟶ **First the brain captures a snapshot of information around us. Then neurons fire up and wire together, leading to fresh memory patterns temporarily stored in the hippocampus and eventually in the furrowed folds of the cortex.**

To make sense of how memories are stored, psychologists had to work out the types of memories that can be stored and what parts of the brain feed this process.

In 1968, Richard Atkinson and Richard Shiffrin proposed three memory stores. Sensory memory stores a fleeting impression of incoming sensory information; short-term memory (STM) can temporarily hold larger chunks of information, while long-term memory (LTM) can permanently store even larger amounts.

Atkinson and Shiffrin's multi-store model hypothesised that information is transferred between sensory, STM and LTM compartments in order, and distant memories can be retrieved and transferred to the short-term store if required.

In 1972, Endel Tulving distinguished different types of LTM, most famously coining the term 'episodic memory' to refer to personally experienced events. This differs from semantic memory, which is focussed on general facts.

Then in 1974, Alan Baddeley updated our theory of STM. Working memory, he proposed, is able to process as well as store information.

To become long-term memory, the brain takes a snapshot of incoming information, then submits it to a series of successive changes and to a stabilisation process called memory consolidation. Studies show that new learning, damage to the hippocampus, or even drugs that block protein synthesis, can disrupt the consolidation of memory.

For most of the 20th century, scientists believed that when the brain made a long-term memory, it was compiling a permanent file; and the process of remembering required the brain to search through the folds of the cortex and dig out the file, before returning it unchanged after use.

However, in the early 21st century, Karim Nader and Joseph LeDoux challenged this idea of permanence with experiments that showed the fragility of memory. According to reconsolidation theory, when we remember an event, the memory trace becomes flexible for a limited time and must be consolidated all over again to be remembered in the future. This means that when we recall an event we rewrite it, and it is the rewritten version that we remember next time. So, although the brain stores memory, it seems these memories can change over time.

TYPES OF MEMORY

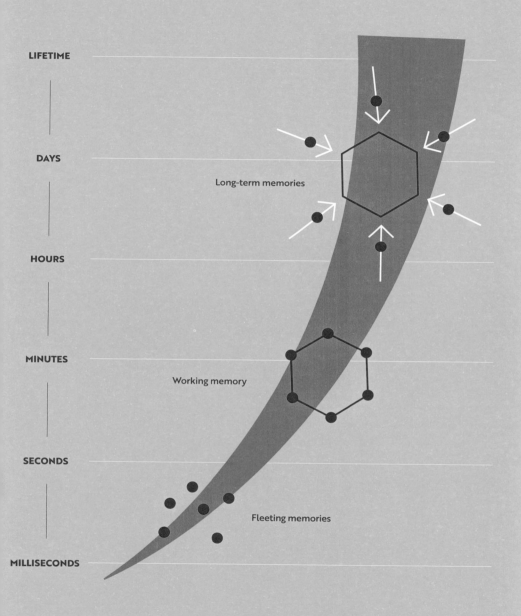

LIFETIME

DAYS

Long-term memories

HOURS

MINUTES

Working memory

SECONDS

Fleeting memories

MILLISECONDS

In simple terms, memory is the storage of information. It runs along a continuum, capturing changes in storage from milliseconds to decades. At one end, fleeting memories, stored for milliseconds, hold our sensory information – what we see, hear, taste, touch and feel – in any given moment.

A little further along the continuum sits working memory or short-term memory, with storage capacity from a few seconds to a few minutes. At the far end rests long-term memory, which can hold information for a lifetime.

Do you groupthink, therefore you err?

→ From business meetings to football crowds, people think and act differently when they're part of a group. Groupthink occurs when the cumulative desire for conformity overrides rational decision making, leading to bad outcomes.

In his dystopian novel *1984*, George Orwell described 'doublethink' – a process by which people are forced to accept conflicting beliefs that are often at odds with their own memories or sense of reality. It later prompted American psychologist Irving Janis to conceive and study groupthink.

Groupthink occurs when individual opinions become drowned out by a collective consensus. Group members fail to consider alternative perspectives because it's often easier to stay quiet and blend in than it is to speak up and stand out. As a result, groups may end up making decisions that are unwise and based on unrealistic assumptions.

The results can be catastrophic. Janis used the 1961 Bay of Pigs invasion (President Kennedy's failed invasion of Castro's Cuba) and the 1941 Japanese attack on Pearl Harbor as prime examples. In both cases, opposing views were ignored and group members endorsed dangerous stereotypes about their enemy. Kennedy's administration presumed Castro's forces would be easily overthrown, while Roosevelt's inner circle rationalised that the Japanese would never dare attack the USA. Janis subsequently formulated his ideas on groupthink in an influential 1972 book.

Groupthink is influenced heavily by cognitive dissonance: the phenomenon whereby it is psychologically stressful to hold two conflicting views at once. Leon Festinger proposed his theory of cognitive dissonance in 1957 after studying a cult. Members believed the world would end in a flood, but when the flood never came, they were forced to revise their views. Hardcore members said that the flood had been prevented by their devotion, whereas fringe members were more likely to accept they had been wrong. Both groups experienced dissonance and found different solutions to the problem.

Festinger proposed that we have an inner drive to hold our beliefs and behaviour in harmony, and to avoid or reduce dissonance, and yet such conflict is rife in our everyday lives. We smoke even though we know it causes lung cancer, we tailgate drivers even though we know it makes us angry and we jet off on holiday even though we know it worsens global warming.

GROUPTHINK

It can be hard to make your voice heard in a group of opposing views. Conflicting opinions can lead to a misalignment of our behaviours with our beliefs, and the emergence of groupthink. This can lead to negative outcomes, including making the wrong decisions, stifling creativity and ignoring moral or ethical consequences of actions or events. Groupthink occurs in everyday scenarios, such as family arguments, but the effects can be especially harmful in military, medical and political situations.

Is the short cut a dangerous route?

⟶ Taking a short cut in decision making can be risky, but we do it all the time, and in some cases it's the best option.

Human beings are smart – we make logical, rational decisions based on a sensible analysis of the available information. Right?

Well, sometimes. But in the 1970s and 1980s, psychologists Daniel Kahneman and Amos Tversky developed a theory that challenged traditional economic ideas. According to prospect theory, we hold a range of unconscious biases and a preference for all kinds of short cuts, which can easily lead us to make irrational decisions.

An example of a bias is that we are very loss-averse. The pain of losing £1,000, say, can only be relieved by the pleasure of gaining much more – even double that amount, according to some studies. Gambling more heavily after a loss shows this bias in action.

In general, we take more decision-making short cuts in situations where we don't have all the information, we're struggling to process that information, or we feel under pressure to act quickly. In these circumstances, a short cut may be our only option, but that isn't always a bad situation.

Kahneman came to describe logical, deliberate thinking – based on a careful and accurate weighing up of pros and cons – as slow, 'system 2', thinking. In some situations, this step-by-step method is clearly best. But when faced with uncertainty or real complexity, we might instead adopt fast, 'system 1', thinking. This type of thinking can be influenced by potentially harmful biases, but it also allows for intuitions.

Intuitions come from implicit knowledge – knowledge that we've gained through experience that becomes automatic, such as knowing how to ride a bicycle. We might not be able to explain this knowledge (and it may well be patchy and imperfect), but we can still use it. Consider a city trader deciding whether to buy or sell a particular stock. It's hard for the trader to make the decision carefully and logically, but intuitions – based on prior experience – can provide a short cut to the right choice.

So, taking a short cut to a decision can be dangerous, but it can also sometimes be the best route to take.

HEURISTICS

NEBRASKA

KANSAS

Heuristics are mental short cuts that reduce cognitive workload but can lead to false conclusions. One form, the 'availability heuristic', is used when making judgements about the frequency of an event. In one commonly cited example, if people are asked whether Kansas or Nebraska has a higher incidence of tornadoes, they are likely to answer 'Kansas' simply because they recall the famous example from the film The Wizard of Oz.

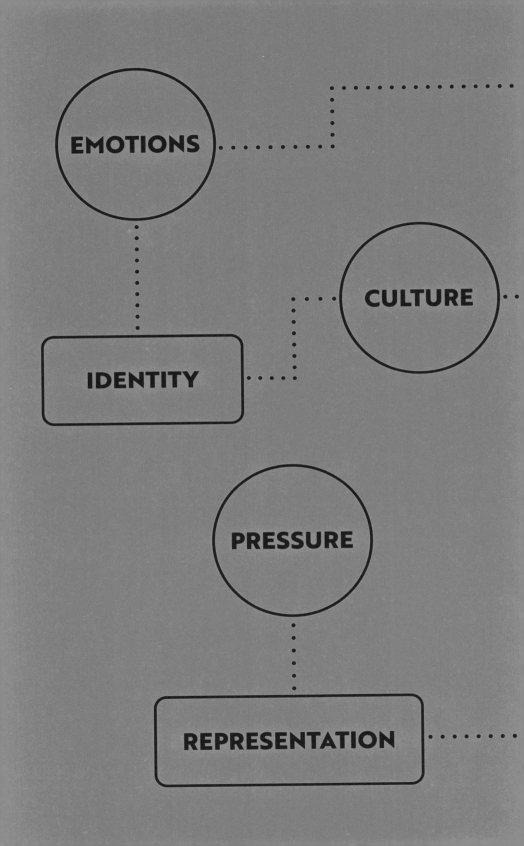

CHAPTER 2

SOCIAL PSYCHOLOGY

CONFORMITY

CONTROL

ENVIRONMENT

INTRODUCTION

On your own, you might risk everything to help someone in trouble. But in a group, your desire to fit in could override your urge to rescue. Getting to grips with the power of groups, how they shape us and why is at the heart of social psychology.

Groups, including our cultural group, can affect how we think and behave, how we feel, and even how we see other people's feelings. Whether our emotions really are written all over our faces is debatable. But there is consensus that our **EMOTIONAL FACIAL EXPRESSIONS** give clues about what we're feeling. Ekman said there were seven core emotions that we experience and see in others: anger, disgust, fear, joy, contempt, sadness and surprise.

Groups can influence whether we'll step up and help someone in need. When we don't, psychologists say that we could be victims of the **BYSTANDER EFFECT**, where the presence of others has discouraged our urge to intervene. Certain group features seem to override this effect. For example, people are more likely to help a woman in distress when all the spectators are women, or to step up if they know many of the people in the group.

You could say that in a group, we act like sheep. **SOLOMON ASCH** in the 1950s called this phenomenon **GROUP CONFORMITY**. It was based on his studies that tested whether people would deliberately give wrong answers if they first heard someone in their group vocalise an incorrect answer. It seems they would.

Choosing what is easier rather than what is best often means surrendering responsibility to authority figures, and is a phenomenon studied during **MILGRAM'S ELECTRIC SHOCK EXPERIMENT**. Milgram observed that giving orders while wearing a lab coat and acting with authority led people to dangerously increase the intensity of what they thought were real electric shocks being delivered to another person.

Perhaps more fascinating is discovering under which conditions we will buck the trend. It seems we're less likely to toe the line with unreasonable orders when they're delivered by someone dressed casually.

HENRI TAJFEL discovered that groups created around flimsy boundaries, such as dot-spotting ability, influence members in similar ways to groups created around meaningful boundaries, such as age or gender. Building on this, Tajfel and Turner coined **SOCIAL IDENTITY THEORY** to explain why people are quick to align themselves with others. They proposed that belonging to a group gives a sense of meaning.

One of the best ways to overcome the bias of favouring those in our group is to experiment with extending compassion to people outside the group. A compassionate stance could also override our tendency to make attribution errors, such as assuming someone's annoying behaviour is a sign they're a bad person rather than a sign of circumstances.

SOCIAL PSYCHOLOGY MAP

PUBLIC CONVERSATION
When a subject is incorporated into everyday knowledge and is widely talked about in common language.

COMMON LANGUAGE
Terms that are widely used and understood; helps us to incorporate complex ideas into everyday life.

COLLECTIVIST CULTURES
Societies in which the greater good of the group as a whole takes precedent over individual needs and desires.

MOSCOVICI'S SOCIAL REPRESENTATIONS
Individuals and societies make sense of difficult concepts by creating alternative versions of them that are easier to relate to.

CHARLES DARWIN
English naturalist, geologist and biologist (1809–82) best known for his theories on evolution. He argued that emotional facial expressions are a result of our shared biology.

EMOTIONAL FACIAL EXPRESSIONS
Darwin believed these are universal and innate. Ekman identified seven basic emotions: anger, contempt, disgust, fear, joy, sadness and surprise.

INGROUP/OUTGROUP BIAS
Aligning with those within your own group/discriminating against those outside of your group – no matter how tenuous the criteria by which the group was formed.

SOCIAL IDENTITY THEORY
People are quick to align themselves with others, as belonging to a group gives a social identity, which provides a sense of meaning (Tajfel and Turner).

HENRI TAJFEL
Polish social psychologist (1919–82) who demonstrated the arbitrary nature of group boundaries in his 'minimal group' experiments in the 1960s.

IDENTITY

CULTURE

SOCIAL INFLUENCES

ENVIRONMENTAL FACTORS
Influences on our behaviour and/ or actions that come from outside sources, such as the circumstances in which we find ourselves.

EDWARD JONES
American psychologist (1926–93) who, in 1967, found that people explained the behaviour of others in terms of traits reflecting something fundamental about them as individuals.

INDIVIDUALIST CULTURES
Societies in which individual needs and desires are prioritised and valued over those of the group as a whole; can be prone to fundamental attribution error.

FUNDAMENTAL ATTRIBUTION ERROR
Overemphasising the effects of a person's individual traits on what they do, and underemphasising the situation they are in or environmental factors.

GROUP CONFORMITY
Following the herd and being swayed by the majority; dependent on factors such as culture, group identity and the political atmosphere of the era.

BYSTANDER EFFECT
The presence of others discourages our urge to intervene. Different features of the group, such as gender and familiarity, will have different effects.

MILGRAM'S ELECTRIC SHOCK EXPERIMENT
Controversial experiment where people surrendered responsibility to an authority figure by increasing the intensity of perceived real electric shocks being delivered to another person.

SOCIAL PRESSURE
The power of a group to influence an individual's judgement, creating group conformity.

SOLOMON ASCH
Polish-American psychologist (1907–96) who, in a set of experiments in the 1950s, examined how and why people conform to those around them.

UPSTANDER
Someone who intervenes rather than stands by; will speak out or act to support an individual or cause.

Do we all experience the same emotions?

→ You would think so, given that we all share the same biology. But, it turns out it's a bit more complicated than that. The emotions we experience – and how we express them – are often shaped by culture.

Emotions are crucial survival tools. They're the body's way of telling us that something in our world has changed and that we need to pay attention to it.

The idea that everyone on Earth experiences the same emotions goes back to Charles Darwin. In 1872, he argued that emotional facial expressions are universal and innate, a result of our shared biology. Since then, scientists have found some evidence to support this. The psychologist Paul Ekman claims to have identified seven basic emotions – anger, contempt, disgust, fear, joy, sadness and surprise – that everyone feels in themselves and recognises in others, regardless of ethnicity, language, culture or where they live.

Recently, though, other researchers have come to a different view. They argue that emotional expression is more complex than Darwin proposed, and that the way we respond to a situation emotionally is influenced by culture. A Westerner's look of disgust may be interpreted by someone from Papua New Guinea as fear. Certain emotional states seem to be specific to certain cultures. Japanese people feel *arigata-meiwaku* when someone does them an unwelcome favour that they are nonetheless obliged to be grateful for. We might all feel this way from time to time, but the Japanese have coined a word for it because in Japan it's important to be respectful to those in your social group, even if it rankles.

Emotions may even be particular to individuals. The state of arousal that one person experiences as terror might be experienced by someone else as excitement. And there is more than one way to feel and express anger or sadness, joy or surprise, contentment or awe. All of this is bound to make communicating with other people a little harder than if emotions were universal. So, perhaps the only way to be sure what someone is feeling when their facial expression changes is to ask them.

EMOTIONAL FACIAL EXPRESSIONS

1. HAPPINESS

2. ANGER

FACES IN REPOSE

3. FEAR

Most of us show our emotions on our faces without even thinking about it. Distinct facial expressions signal the common ones. For example, raised cheeks, wrinkling around the corners of the eyes and a broad smile suggest happiness (1). Tight lips, wide eyes and eyebrows pulled down or together denote anger (2); while the face of fear is linked to raised upper eyelids and eyebrows, and lips stretched backwards (3). If you try enacting these expressions, you may well feel the corresponding emotions.

Would you step in to stop a murder?

→ We all like to think we would. But our chosen course of action depends on several factors, the most important being the number of people we're with – and who they are.

It sounds counterintuitive, but it seems that being a Good Samaritan is a lot more difficult in the presence of others. This phenomenon is known as the bystander effect, and it has mystified psychologists for decades. The bystander effect came to light after the murder of a 28-year-old woman called Kitty Genovese in Queens, New York, in 1964. *The New York Times* reported that 38 people witnessed the attack without doing anything to stop it. This was an exaggeration, but since then many experimental studies have found that the effect is largely true – with some important caveats.

Why would the presence of others discourage us from helping? There are several possible reasons. We might assume or hope that someone else will take responsibility. We might be worried about appearing incompetent in front of a crowd. Or we might do what people often do in unfamiliar situations and take our cue from those around us; after all, if no one else is reacting, why should we?

Bystander passivity appears to be more pronounced in some situations than others, with gender and familiarity playing key roles. For example, an individual is more likely to step in when the victim and all the spectators are female. A man is more likely to step in when he is the only male in the group. And intervention in general is much more likely if all the bystanders know one another and are part of a cohesive group.

Is there anything we can do to improve our chances of helping – of being an upstander rather than a bystander? One tactic could be to try to view the victim as part of our own social group, or to focus on the things we have in common with them. Human nature being what it is, we may be more inclined to take a risk and act if we think the person in trouble is 'one of us'.

BYSTANDERS VS UPSTANDERS

Friends can be empowering in all kinds of situations, even dangerous ones. Few of us will step forward to help someone in distress if we're in a crowd of strangers. Among friends, however, there is often no shortage of potential heroes. Being surrounded by people we know and trust appears to increase our sense of social responsibility and makes us more determined to help those in need.

Are humans just sheep?

→ **That's a bit unfair to sheep, which are cleverer than they're given credit for. It's true that humans do sometimes follow one another without thinking, but there's usually a good reason for it.**

The popular idea that people conform to what those around them are doing or thinking stems from a set of experiments conducted by the American psychologist Solomon Asch in the 1950s. Asch was interested in how social pressure can influence a person's judgement. He invited volunteers to his lab, where they joined a group of seven others, all of whom – unbeknown to the volunteers – were colleagues of Asch. He presented the group with two large cards. One of the cards showed a single vertical line; the other showed three lines of various lengths, one of which was identical to the line on the first card. He then asked each group member to pick out the line that matched.

This should have been easy – on their own, the volunteers would almost certainly have answered correctly every time. But in twelve out of eighteen rounds, Asch had his colleagues call out wrong answers, deliberately choosing lines that were clearly longer or shorter than the reference line. Over those twelve rounds, 76 per cent of the volunteers answered incorrectly at least once, ignoring their better judgement and conforming to the (false) opinion of the majority.

Asch's experiment has been repeated many times under different conditions. The results suggest that although group conformity is a real phenomenon, it is dependent on factors such as culture, the identity of the group and even the political atmosphere of the era. For example, people in collectivist cultures such as China and Japan conform more than those in individualistic cultures such as Europe and the USA. Volunteers who identify strongly with the rest of their group (in terms of age or ethnicity, for instance) are also more likely to fall into line. Levels of conformity appear to be lower today than in the 1950s – at least in the USA – possibly because modern societies are less conservative and students are more questioning.

In some ways it would be surprising if we didn't conform under group pressure. We are social beings, after all, and standing alone can be risky. It takes courage.

SOCIAL PRESSURE EXPERIMENT

The question that Asch asked volunteers in his social pressure experiment was simple: which of the lines A, B or C matches the target line? The answer is C. But when Asch's colleagues in the group deliberately answered incorrectly, three-quarters of the volunteers did likewise, allowing themselves to be persuaded rather than trusting their own opinion. In a situation like this, it's almost impossible to predict how each of us will react.

At what point do you stop following orders?

→ It depends on who's giving them. Our inclination to obey authority can lead us to do things we disagree with, but circumstances and the people involved can have a big influence on our choices.

You've probably heard of Stanley Milgram's electric shock experiment. It's one of the most famous in psychology. Like many of his colleagues during the 1950s and 60s, Milgram was profoundly influenced by the atrocities of the Second World War. So he devised an experiment to try to understand why normal people do dreadful things. It didn't quite answer that question, but it taught us a lot about when people obey orders – and when they don't.

Here's how it worked. Milgram told his volunteers that the experiment was designed to test the effects of punishment on learning. The volunteers were assigned the role of 'teacher': their job was to deliver an electric shock to a 'learner' whenever the learner misremembered a word from a list of word pairs. In reality, the learner was Milgram's collaborator and never received a shock, but his fake cries of pain persuaded the teacher that the shocks were working.

The experimenter, who donned a white coat and an air of authority, encouraged the volunteers to increase the voltage after every wrong answer. To Milgram's astonishment, two-thirds of them did, right up to the maximum 450 volts, far beyond the point at which the learner appeared to lose consciousness. This result is often taken as evidence that people tend to automatically surrender responsibility for their actions to authority figures, even when they disapprove of the outcome. But the baseline experiment didn't convey the full picture. Milgram carried out more than 30 lesser-known variations of his experiment, which produced rather different results.

For example, the volunteers were far less obedient when the experimenter was not in the room but gave orders remotely; or when the experiment was carried out in an industrial city rather than the august surroundings of an Ivy League university; or when the experimenter put aside his white coat and appeared more ordinary; or when the volunteer was joined by another who refused to continue. This suggests that our tendency to follow orders depends very strongly on context.

MILGRAM'S SHOCK EXPERIMENT

Milgram used a simple set-up for his electric shock experiment. The volunteer (the 'teacher') was asked to read a list of word pairs to the 'learner', for example, blue box, nice day, wild duck, which the learner then had to recall. Each time the learner made a mistake, the teacher flicked a switch, which they believed gave the learner an electric shock. The voltage was meant to increase with each error, and the experimenter was on hand to encourage, impel or order the teacher to continue whenever they hesitated. The voltages ranged from 15 to 450 in 15-volt steps. How far would you go?

Is it all about 'us' and 'them'?

⟶ At one level it is. Group living shapes just about everything we do, and ingroup favouritism seems inevitable. But it doesn't have to lead to war.

Human beings evolved to live in groups, and it's almost impossible to avoid that impulse. We instinctively categorise ourselves with others who we think are similar to us, along the lines of background, race, nationality, religion, age, gender and so on, and favour them over those who we think are different.

It doesn't take much to create a sense of 'us' and 'them'. We do it on the slightest of pretexts, such as the length of someone's hair or the colour of their eyes. The psychologist Henri Tajfel demonstrated the arbitrary nature of group boundaries in his 'minimal group' experiments at the University of Bristol in the 1960s. He found that people would readily discriminate against others based on something as trivial as whether they overestimated or underestimated the number of dots on a screen. Outgroup bias is extraordinarily easy to trigger, he concluded.

Tajfel and his colleague John Turner went on to develop social identity theory to explain why people are so quick to align themselves with others. They believed that being part of a group helps us define who we are, and that this social identity gives us a sense of meaning. Furthermore, social identities are hugely influential to our behaviour and thinking. They are also transient: we can belong to many different groups, and we might behave differently with each of them.

It can feel great to be part of a group. The flipside is that it can harden our hearts towards those who don't belong. Group prejudice has played a role in almost all conflicts. Prejudice is not inevitable, though: ingroup bias can exist without outgroup hostility. It's possible to feel a profound sense of loyalty towards one's own group and at the same time stay friendly with outsiders – in other words, you can be a fan of Liverpool F.C. but still hang out with fans of Manchester City. But this approach requires tolerance and an acceptance that other people's ways may be different to our own – which is perhaps the biggest challenge of our age.

THE 'MINIMAL GROUP' EXPERIMENTS

Tajfel tested his ideas about social prejudice by dividing several dozen pupils from a local school into two groups. He determined the groups on deliberately flimsy criteria, such as whether they underestimated or overestimated the number of dots on a screen. He then asked each pupil to distribute a sum of money among their schoolmates. To Tajfel's surprise, the majority of pupils gave more money to those who were members of their seemingly meaningless group: dot underestimators discriminated in favour of their fellow underestimators.

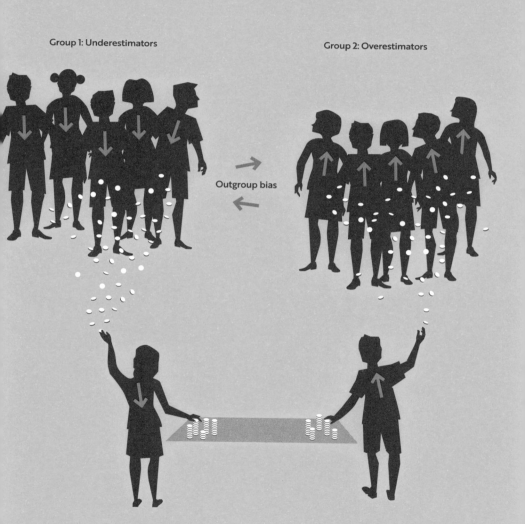

Group 1: Underestimators

Group 2: Overestimators

Outgroup bias

How do ideas enter the mainstream?

⟶ Scientific ideas pass through a social filter that makes them more palatable and easier to share, allowing us all to be armchair experts on complex issues such as the multiverse or genetic modification.

There has always been a tension between scientific ideas and how those ideas are understood by the public. To those of us without an academic background, scientific theories can seem impenetrable and mysterious. Nonetheless, many of them end up being incorporated into everyday knowledge and become part of the public conversation. We don't need a degree in biology to understand the basic principle of the selfish gene, for example, and to pontificate about it among our friends.

The French social psychologist Serge Moscovici spent a good part of his career exploring how this assimilation of complex thinking into ordinary understanding happens. He believed that individuals and societies make sense of difficult concepts by creating alternative versions of them that are easier to relate to. He called these versions social representations. Social representations 'help make the unfamiliar familiar', as Moscovici put it. They can be described using language that everyone can understand, rather than the often arcane jargon of academia. Crucially, they allow societies to discuss and make decisions about ideas that otherwise would seem out of reach.

Moscovici developed his theories in Paris in the 1960s while focussing on psychoanalysis. He chose psychoanalysis because it was a controversial academic discipline that was nonetheless popular among non-professionals in France at the time. To discuss its methods and principles, it was necessary to translate them into language that could be commonly understood. Moscovici noticed that people talked about psychoanalysis in ways that evoked their own everyday experiences, such as comparing a psychoanalytic interview with a religious confession.

Social representations of scientific ideas are especially important today, at a time when we're dealing with existential issues such as climate change and biodiversity loss. Such issues used to be confined to the pages of academic journals, but the development of a common language around them has allowed us to incorporate them into daily thinking – and to push for action on a global scale.

SOCIAL REPRESENTATION

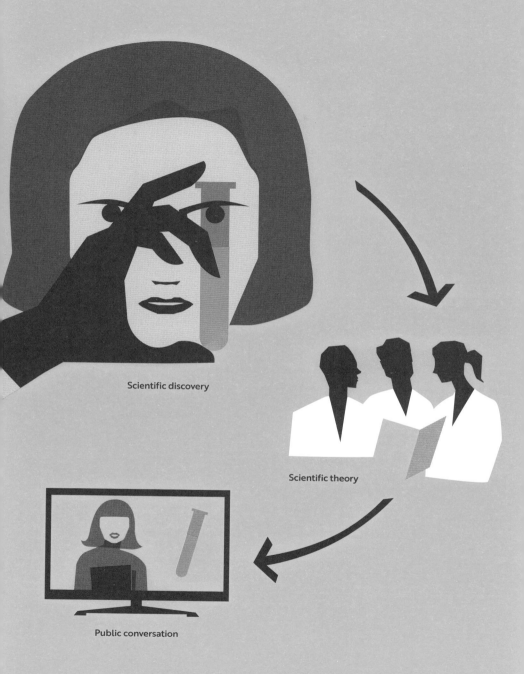

Scientific discovery

Scientific theory

Public conversation

Moscovici's theory of social representations explains how scientific discoveries and theories are translated into concepts that the general population can easily understand and discuss. While scientists might focus on the mechanisms of and theory behind a discovery, the public conversation revolves around the potential impact on everyday lives.

Why did you do that?

⟶ **If someone does something bad, we tend to assume that this tells us something fundamental about them, and that they must be a bad person. But we're often wrong.**

Imagine that you make a call to your bank to ask about your overdraft, and the person answering the phone is inexplicably offhand or patronising. Your immediate reaction might be 'What a rude person!' In other words, you assume that their behaviour reflects the kind of person they are.

This would be a perfectly normal response, but chances are you will have committed what psychologists call the fundamental attribution error. This is the tendency to overemphasise the effects of a person's individual traits on what they do, and to underemphasise the situation they are in. While personality traits and temperament do influence the way we behave, these characteristics are often trumped by environmental factors, such as the circumstances we find ourselves in. The bank worker who dismissed you on the phone is unlikely to be a sociopath. It's more probable they've had to deal with a pressured situation such as a hectic journey to work.

The fundamental attribution error became a prominent idea in social psychology after an experiment led by Edward Jones in 1967. Jones found that people explained the behaviour of others in terms of traits presumed to reflect something fundamental about them as a person, even when their behaviour clearly linked to events outside their control. Later experiments found that the fundamental attribution error is influenced by culture, and that people from individualistic cultures are more prone to it than those from collectivist cultures.

One explanation for why we're prone to attribution errors is the possibility that they increase our sense of control over our lives. If everyone is fully responsible for what they do, it makes it easy to apportion blame and believe in a just world. The idea that behaviour is unpredictable and shaped by an ever-changing environment is unsettling. But if we got our heads around it, it could result in everyone being a little more forgiving.

THE FUNDAMENTAL ATTRIBUTION ERROR

The fundamental attribution error first came to light in a classic experiment by Jones and Harris. They asked volunteers to read essays that supported or criticised Fidel Castro, then had them assess the writers' attitudes towards the Cuban leader. When the volunteers were told that the writers were free to choose their own positions, they generally rated those who had written supportive essays as pro-Castro, as you'd expect. But when told an instructor had given the writers which position to take, they still assumed that the essays reflected their true beliefs. They appeared to discount vital information: the writers' choices had been made for them.

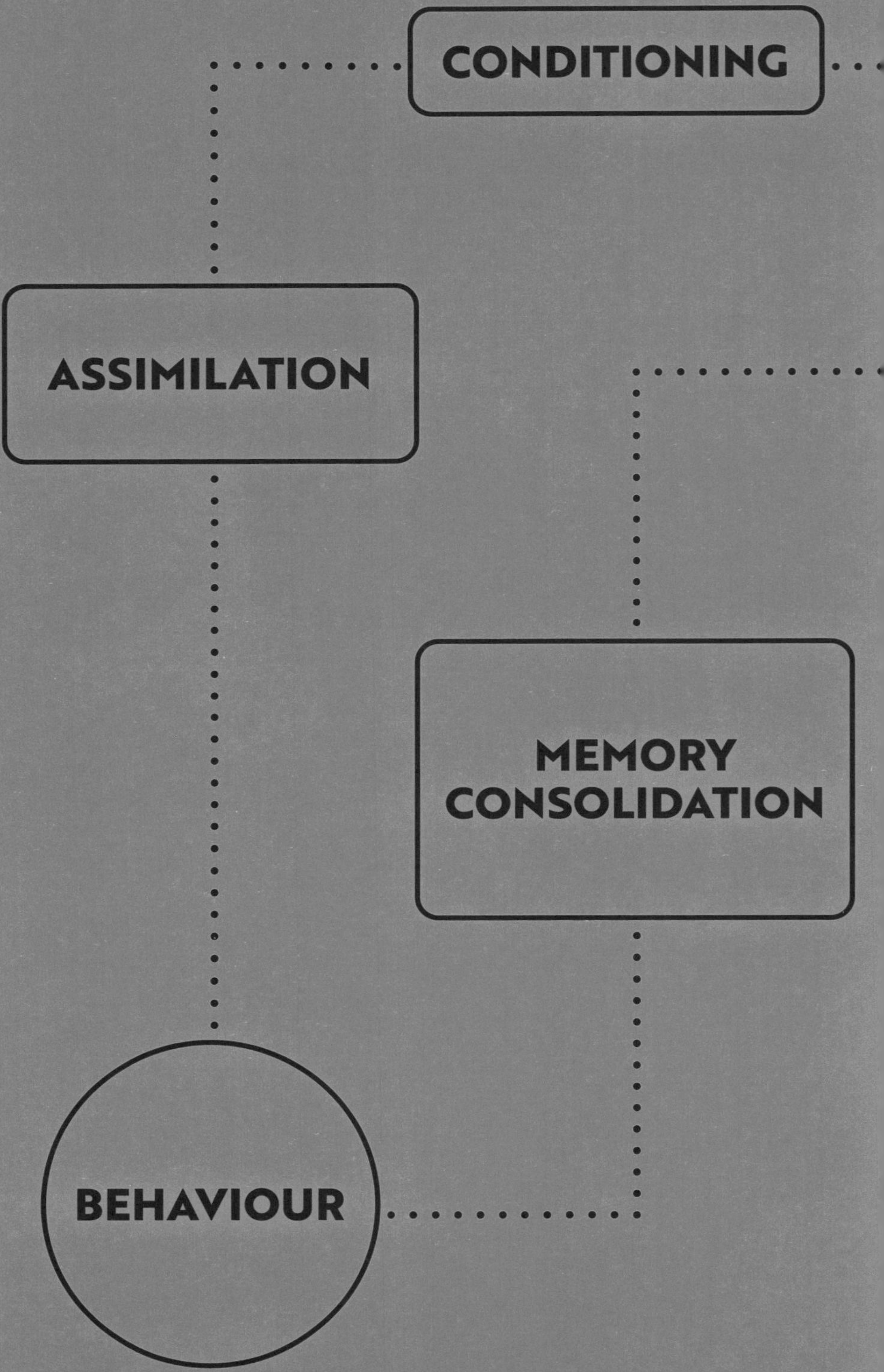
CONDITIONING
ASSIMILATION
MEMORY CONSOLIDATION
BEHAVIOUR

CHAPTER 3

LEARNING

ACCOMMODATION

PROCESSING

SCHEMA

INTRODUCTION

Bench pressing might fortify your muscles, but it's learning new skills that makes neurons sprout and strengthen. From infancy to adulthood, what and how we learn is at the core of how we behave. This chapter delves deep into the most groundbreaking findings psychology has to offer about how and why we learn the way we do.

Behaviourism, coined by Watson in the early 1900s, saw the value in nurture over nature when it comes to learning. Making links was seen as pivotal to how we form the habits that satisfy and drive us, from exercising to smoking. **IVAN PAVLOV** discovered he could teach a dog to salivate at the sound of a bell by ringing the bell before feeding time. The dog learned that the ring meant food was on its way and began to salivate on hearing it. Coined **CLASSICAL CONDITIONING**, this form of learning occurs when we link two unrelated stimuli.

Reward and punishment are other essential ways we learn, which **B.F. SKINNER** called **OPERANT CONDITIONING**. Behaviours that are rewarded are more likely to be repeated. So, if your spouse takes the bins out and you reward them with a kind word or a deliciously cooked dinner, you're helping them learn that good things happen when they remove the rubbish, and they'll be more likely to do it again. The theory says we should be able to unlearn a behaviour by ceasing the rewards or linking the behaviour to punishments.

Children learn a lot about how to behave through conditioning, and a lot about communication through imitation. **BANDURA'S SOCIAL LEARNING THEORY** proposed to account for the processes required for a behaviour to be copied effectively, such as attention, memory and motivation. But it was **PIAGET'S THEORY OF COGNITIVE DEVELOPMENT** that described how children make sense of the world on their route to adulthood. Toddlers will struggle with understanding what other people think, but they are phenomenal at language learning. Chomsky proposed that's because they have ready access to processes in the brain that come together to form a **LANGUAGE ACQUISITION DEVICE**, which seems to stiffen around the age of eighteen, making language-learning much tougher.

GLADWELL'S 10,000-HOUR RULE favours practice over talent on the journey to elite performance, but it fails to take account of quality of practice, luck and raw talent as contributors to success.

Psychology offers tools to boost our learning, with tips to strengthen our focus, thinking and recollections. Deeper processing leads to better memory, a finding attributed to Craik and Tulving. **MNEMONICS** – linking a fact, image or story to something we want to remember, or creating an anagram – can help too, improving memory by almost 50 per cent.

LEARNING MAP

CONDITIOING

IVAN PAVLOV
Soviet-Russian physiologist (1849–1936) known for his work on classical conditioning, and his salivating dog experiment (1897) in particular.

CONDITIONED RESPONSES
Emotions become learned responses to previously neutral stimuli, as shown in Watson and Rayner's 1920 study of rats presented alongside loud noises to scare a baby.

CLASSICAL CONDITIONING
Behaviourists such as Watson and Pavlov said we learn behaviours through a process of making links; that a particular stimulus can produce a certain response.

OPERANT CONDITIONING
Rewards strengthen, change or motivate behaviours; learning is through reinforcement or punishment, with behaviour controlled by its consequences (Skinner).

REINFORCEMENT SCHEDULES
The delivery of rewards according to a set of rules, which can affect response rates and extinction rates of behaviour.

B.F. SKINNER
American behaviourist (1904–90) who developed theories on conditioning and behaviourism. Famous for his work on operant conditioning and his notorious 'Skinner's box' rat experiment.

ASSIMILATION
One of the two ways (see also *accommodation*) in which new information fits around or expands existing schema; when information is morphed to fit existing schemas (Piaget).

ACCOMMODATION
One of the two ways (see also *assimilation*) in which new information fits around or expands existing schema; when schemas are updated with new information (Piaget).

REHEARSAL

GLADWELL'S 10,000-HOUR RULE
Repeated practice for at least ten years, rather than natural talent, strengthens neural connections, making recall of rehearsed information or skills more likely.

MNEMONICS
Mental systems or devices to assist memory, such as linking a fact, image or story to something we want to remember or creating an anagram.

ELABORATIVE REHEARSAL
Memory and learning technique that involves a meaningful analysis of information during deep processing by applying association, organisation/categorisation or mnemonic strategies.

MILLER'S INFORMATION PROCESSING THEORY
The human mind has four processing stages: 1) attending to information, 2) encoding it, 3) storing it in the memory system, 4) retrieving it later.

CRITICAL PERIOD HYPOTHESIS
The idea that there is a time when we are sensitive to linguistic stimuli, but beyond this, it may be too late to learn a language with fluency.

BANDURA'S SOCIAL LEARNING THEORY
We observe then imitate behaviour, with conditions, such as rewards, tempting our efforts.

PIAGET'S THEORY OF COGNITIVE DEVELOPMENT
Children's intelligence changes as they grow through four key stages. As they develop, they acquire new schemas and expand old ones.

MEDIATION PROCESSES
The attention we give to observed behaviour, the ability to reproduce it and the motivation to perform it.

CHOMSKY'S LANGUAGE ACQUISITION DEVICE (LAD)
The LAD consists of innate language principles and allows us to construct an understanding of grammar and language when we hear languages around us.

COGNITIVE DEVELOPMENT

Do you salivate at the dinner bell?

→ If you do, it may be the result of classical conditioning. Pavlov's iconic studies, in which dogs salivated at the sound of bells, provided us with some of the most influential ideas about human behaviour and learning.

Why do we behave the way we do? Behaviourists such as John B. Watson said we learn our behaviours through a process of making links. He called this form of learning classical conditioning.

Watson's ideas were largely based on the observations of Ivan Pavlov. Originally a physiologist, Pavlov was studying the salivation of dogs in response to being fed when he made an accidental discovery. He noticed that the dogs would often salivate before the food was presented – for instance, when they heard the assistant's footsteps coming towards them.

Propelled by these observations, Pavlov published a number of now-iconic psychological studies in 1897. Famously, he repeatedly placed a bowl of food in front of dogs while ringing a bell. Although dogs naturally respond to food with salivation, they have no natural salivation response to ringing bells. However, after a number of repeated pairings of the food and the bell, the dogs had learned through association; they began salivating when they heard the bell, even though there

was no food in front of them. This is classical conditioning: a learning process that occurs when two stimuli are repeatedly paired until the subject's natural reaction to the second stimulus is elicited by the first stimulus alone.

Intrigued by Pavlov's studies, Watson extended the findings, strongly siding with nurture over nature. He believed conditioned-based learning shapes the ways in which we behave, including how we feel. Watson and Rayner's study (1920), though unethical, was pioneering in applying classical conditioning to human behaviour and emotion. The study presented a rat alongside loud noises to a baby called Little Albert. These noises made the baby cry. When the conditioning period ended, Little Albert had a fear of rats. The study illustrated that emotions could become conditioned responses. Though Watson's hard-line behaviourist stance and favoured conditioning paradigm have both since been debated and reworked, his theoretical and experimental findings are still successfully applied to psychological topics such as phobias and education.

PAVLOV'S DOG EXPERIMENT

In Pavlov's model of classical conditioning, food is considered the unconditioned stimulus, because it naturally arouses an automatic, unconditioned response in the dog: salivation. The bell is a neutral stimulus, as it produces no automatic responses until it is paired repeatedly with the unconditioned stimulus (food). Then the bell becomes a conditioned stimulus. It will evoke a conditioned response – salivation – when presented alone.

Can we learn from our rewards?

→ Yes! We can. Operant conditioning suggests that rewards can strengthen, change or motivate behaviours, whether they're healthy (a stroll after a stint of hard work) or unhealthy (a cake-break).

B.F. Skinner was a behaviourist who added nuance to Pavlov's and Watson's pioneering ideas of conditioning and behaviourism (see page 54). Unlike Watson, Skinner believed in nature as well as nurture; that is, human behaviour can be innate, learned or a combination of the two. Nevertheless, Skinner still asserted that we learn our behaviours, and this learning is best explained through the paradigm of operant conditioning, which is learning through reinforcement or punishment. Behaviour is controlled by its consequences. Put simply: if our actions are rewarded, they are more likely to be repeated, and vice versa. Reinforcement works to increase behaviour; punishment works to decrease behaviour.

Skinner differentiated between positive and negative reinforcements and punishments. Let's say your boss wants you to make a certain amount of sales each week. They could use positive reinforcement by rewarding you with extra commission for reaching this amount, or they could use negative reinforcement by taking away from your commission when the goal is not met.

Ferster and Skinner (1957) introduced the idea of reinforcement schedules: the delivery of rewards according to a set of rules. They found they could affect response rates (the repetition rate of reward-seeking behaviour) and extinction rates (the rate at which this behaviour dies out). For instance, a variable ratio schedule, in which a reward is delivered after an unpredictable number of responses, produced the slowest rate of extinction. This can be seen in gambling, where people desire to play the same slot machine countless times, knowing their reward could come at any point. Continuous reinforcement, in which a reward is given to every response, has a slow response rate and a fast extinction rate. This may be because responders become quickly satisfied, negating the need for more responses.

Skinner went on to use his principles of operant conditioning to develop methods of shaping behaviour. Today, Skinner's work has applications in the explanation of topics such as addiction, as well as practical applications in places such as classrooms and prisons.

CONDITIONING IN THE SKINNER BOX

Skinner most famously studied operant conditioning by placing rats in a 'Skinner box'. For positive reinforcement, pressing the lever released food pellets. After accidentally pressing it a number of times, the rats eventually learned to go straight to the lever when placed in the box. For negative reinforcement, Skinner subjected the rats to an electric current, which they learned to turn off by pressing the lever.

Is learning behaviour an imitation game?

⟶ **Albert Bandura says it is. His work focussed on how we learn behaviours from other people. His social learning theory says that children watch then copy behaviour, with conditions such as rewards tempting their efforts.**

The work of Pavlov, Watson and Skinner laid down the groundwork for behaviourism. Psychologist Albert Bandura agreed with the principles of their approach. Yet his work departed from his peers by suggesting that human learning was more than discovering links between stimuli or receiving rewards or punishments. He said humans can learn automatically through observation. In Bandura's framework, children observe models – individuals performing social behaviour – and may respond with imitation. Of course, children do not go around imitating every behaviour they observe – imitation is selective.

Bandura pointed to a host of factors that make imitation more likely. These include perceiving the person you're about to copy as more similar to yourself (e.g. gender), reinforcement (e.g. praise) and what he called vicarious reinforcement – seeing the person you're about to copy receive rewards for their behaviour. Children are also likely to adopt behaviours of someone whom they see as having a lot of desirable qualities.

Bandura's social learning theory (SLT), published in 1977, says that we learn social behaviour by observing other people and imitating their actions. He extended behaviourism, incorporating the idea that humans are active information processors who think about the consequences of their actions. Our thinking can strengthen or weaken the relationship between what we see and what we do. This is called mediation. Bandura noted a number of mediation processes that determine whether or not what we see will change what we do: the attention we give to the behaviour we see, the ability to reproduce it and the motivation to perform it.

Bandura's work has wide-ranging applications. For instance, his Bobo doll experiment (1961) provided insight into the effects of exposing children to violent media. His work also shed light on the development of gender roles, how we create social change and how we make sense of our culture. However, SLT was criticised for not accounting for the cognitive control people have over their behaviours. Bandura created a revised theory, social cognitive theory, in 1986 to better incorporate ideas of human agency.

BANDURA'S BOBO DOLL EXPERIMENT

Bandura's famous experiment had children watch an adult model interact with a Bobo doll. The children watched an aggressive or pleasant interaction, or, in the control group, no interaction. The experimenters then observed each child's subsequent dealings with the doll. Overall, those who watched the aggressive interaction were the most likely to imitate aggressive behaviour, demonstrating that children can learn social behaviour through observation.

Will 10,000 hours of practice make you a genius?

→ Not quite – but they might get you close. Gladwell's enticing rule is that what makes an elite, expert performer is hard work – intense and methodological practice for at least ten years, or 10,000 hours.

Malcolm Gladwell's 10,000-hour rule (2008) says there are no naturals when it comes to talent. Gladwell was inspired by Simon and Chase's 1973 paper on the skill of chess players. The pair concluded that skilled chess playing comes from building up recognition memory of chess patterns through years of practice. They noted that there was not a single grandmaster who had dedicated less than ten years to the game before receiving the title.

The 10,000-hour rule was given a more formal grounding with Ericsson and his colleagues' 1993 study of violinists. They found that the differences in skill between performers were closely tied to their levels of practice, and top-ranked violinists had practised intensely for at least ten years, or an average of 10,000 hours.

So why does practice make perfect? The answer lies in the process of memory consolidation. The human brain contains approximately 100 billion neurons. As in a crowded forest, it takes some work to establish a well-worn pathway between neurons. As neurons repeatedly fire together, they wire together. Therefore, repeated practice strengthens neural connections, and you become more likely to recall the information or skills you have rehearsed.

More recently, Gladwell's rule has come under some criticism. Macnamara and Maitra (2019) repeated Ericsson et al.'s study but could not replicate the results. Though the less skilful violinists did practise for under 10,000 hours, there was almost no difference in hours between the good and the elite (each group averaging about 11,000). Hours spent practising accounted for only a quarter of the difference in violin skills, compared to Ericsson's 48 per cent.

Gladwell himself concedes that other factors – quality of practice, privilege, luck and innate talent – can play a role in success. More recent studies show that 10,000 hours is not a silver bullet for achieving elite status. Nevertheless, it remains clear that dedicated practice does facilitate your rise to the top.

10,000-HOUR RULE

Simon and Chase's study estimated that chess players spent between 10,000 and 50,000 hours studying chess to become grandmasters. Gladwell's use of this example is intentional, as the 10,000-hour rule should only be applied to cognitively demanding fields like chess, which requires a long list of possibilities to be learned to achieve mastery, unlike physically demanding fields like running.

How does a child see the world?

→ According to Piaget, children see the world through the lens of building blocks of knowledge, which stack together to construct their overall understanding of their surroundings. As they develop, so do their building blocks.

Jean Piaget thought babies were born without awareness that a reality exists outside of themselves. Essentially, children act like mini scientists, performing experiments in order to construct a mental model of the world. These models provide a framework for understanding the world around them.

Piaget's theory of cognitive development suggests that children are not less intelligent than adults: rather, their intelligence changes as they grow. The theory proposes four stages of cognitive development: the sensorimotor stage (ages 0–2), the preoperational stage (2–7), the concrete operational stage (7–11) and the formal operational stage (12+) (see page 96).

So, what exactly changes about children's intelligence as they develop? The answer to this is what Piaget calls schema. These are cognitive building blocks: 'units' of knowledge that relate to various aspects of the world, such as objects, actions or concepts. As we develop as human beings, we acquire new schemas and expand old ones.

Piaget described two core ways in which we scaffold new information to fit around or to expand existing schema. These processes help children to progress through his proposed developmental stages. The first is assimilation, in which we morph information to fit existing schemas. For example, a young child may point and shout, 'Puppy!' when seeing a wolf on TV for the first time.

The second is accommodation. This is where great leaps in learning can occur as schemas are updated with new information. So, the child's parent might explain that the animal they see is a wolf not a puppy. As such, the child will be able to change the parameters of their 'puppy' schema by adding that puppies are small and domesticated, and will create a separate schema for wolves.

Though the parameters of Piaget's stages have been challenged, Piaget nevertheless provided a useful and influential framework for understanding children's cognitive development – one which has spawned numerous influential studies.

THE A-NOT-B ERROR

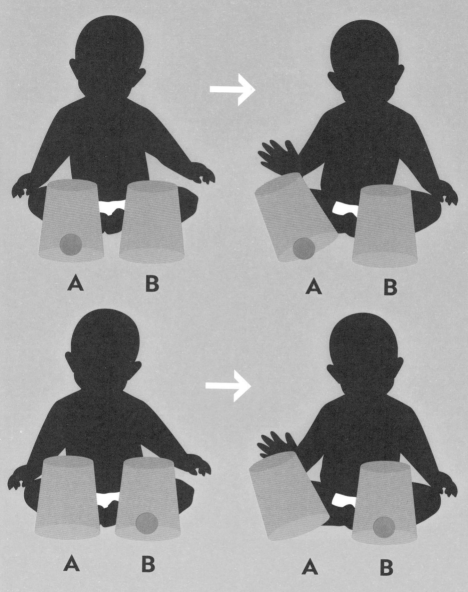

Piaget's experiments demonstrated a phenomenon known as the A-not-B error, typically occurring during the sensorimotor stage. A 9- to 12-month-old sees an object, which is hidden in location 'A'. The child then searches in location A. After this is repeated, the object is hidden in location 'B'. However, the baby still searches in location A. The error illustrates an incomplete schema of object permanence: the understanding that objects still exist even when you cannot see them.

When should you bid *au revoir* to language learning?

⟶ Proponents of the critical period hypothesis suggest anywhere between ages seven and eighteen. Regardless of the specific age, as we get older, our ability to learn languages diminishes significantly.

For young children to learn something as complicated as language with such ease is an incredible feat. Yet almost every child on earth learns a language of some kind – and they seem to be much better equipped for the task than many adults. It's almost as if children were born to do it.

Noam Chomsky suggests that we are, indeed, born to learn languages. In 1969, he theorised that humans possess a language acquisition device (LAD), made up of innate language principles: restricted possibilities within which a language can work. The LAD allows learners to construct an understanding of grammar and language based on raw input from their environment. Simply by hearing languages around us we're able to rapidly acquire a fluency in our young years.

But what happens if we are not exposed to a language until later in life, therefore lacking the LAD's needed input? The critical period hypothesis says that there is a window of time where we are highly sensitive to linguistic stimuli, but beyond this period, it may be too late to learn a language with fluency. That is, at a certain age, the gateway to the LAD may shut.

Many psychologists and linguists have hypothesised about when this critical period ends, with most suggesting that it is around the start of puberty. In the hopes of finding a more definitive answer, a 2018 MIT study by Hartshorne, Tenenbaum and Pinker used the largest dataset for a study of its kind – nearly 670,000 people. They found that the critical period extends well beyond what we thought – up to seventeen or eighteen years old. However, a native-like fluency will likely not be achieved unless children start learning the language by age ten.

So, should adults give up on language learning? Not necessarily. Though fluency may be unlikely, languages can still be learned with competency. Furthermore, Singleton (1995) notes that 5 per cent of adult bilinguals master a second language well into adulthood. However, this learning requires hard work – though it can still be done, the ease of childhood language learning is lost with age.

INFANT LANGUAGE ACQUISITION

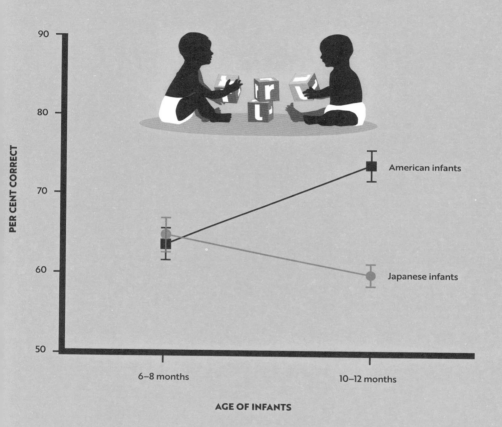

Figure axes:
- Y-axis: PER CENT CORRECT (50, 60, 70, 80, 90)
- X-axis: AGE OF INFANTS (6–8 months, 10–12 months)
- American infants
- Japanese infants

Kuhl and her team demonstrated that even the first year of life is key in shaping our language-learning abilities. The study compared Japanese and American infants' ability to perceive the contrast between 'r' and 'l'. This comparison was used because Japanese-speaking adults cannot distinguish between 'r' and 'l', whereas English-speaking adults can. At 6 to 8 months, Kuhl's infants were equally competent in discriminating the sounds. However, by 12 months, the American infants were much better at discriminating the sounds than the Japanese infants. These data illustrate a critical period for discriminating certain sounds.

Can you hack your memory?

⟶ Well, sort of. While there's no quick fix for improving how well we memorise information, psychology has shown us that we can be much more successful if we put in extra effort through deep processing and mnemonics.

The human mind's capacity to store new information is unlimited. So how can it be so hard to remember the things we need to? Psychological research has shown us that we can streamline our memorising efforts by approaching what we need to learn with intention.

To understand how we can improve our memorising skills, we first have to understand how the mind processes information. George Miller's information processing theory proposed that the human mind has four processing stages. The learner attends to the information being presented to them, and then encodes, or takes in, the information they paid attention to and deem important. This information is then stored in the memory system, in order to be retrieved at a later point.

However, not all processing is created equal. Craik and Lockhart (1972) differentiated between shallow processing – encoding the physical properties or sounds of something – with deep processing – an encoding of meanings. Craik and Tulving's (1975) experiment illustrated the importance of deep processing by asking participants to process target words at different levels of encoding. The shallow processing condition had participants judge whether a word had upper-case or lower-case letters. In the deep processing condition, participants determined whether inserting the word into a blank space in a sentence properly fit its meaning. In a subsequent recall task, the shallow processers achieved 25 per cent recall, whereas 75 per cent was achieved by the deep processers.

What exactly does deep processing entail? Broadly, it involves elaborative rehearsal: a more meaningful analysis of information. For instance, you might attach a fact to a piece of imagery, incorporate it into a story, associate it with other facts or turn it into an anagram. These are all tools called mnemonics: mental systems or devices intended to assist memory. Bower (1972) gave students a list of words to memorise, and found that those who used mnemonics remembered an average of 44 per cent more than those who did not. Furthermore, the way we practise our mnemonics makes a difference: many studies have found that participants do better when their studying process involves a practice test. This allows for deeper encoding, and for participants to assess the quality of their mnemonics.

So, next time you've got a big speech to memorise or exam to prepare for, remember: the magic is in the encoding.

INFORMATION PROCESSING THEORY

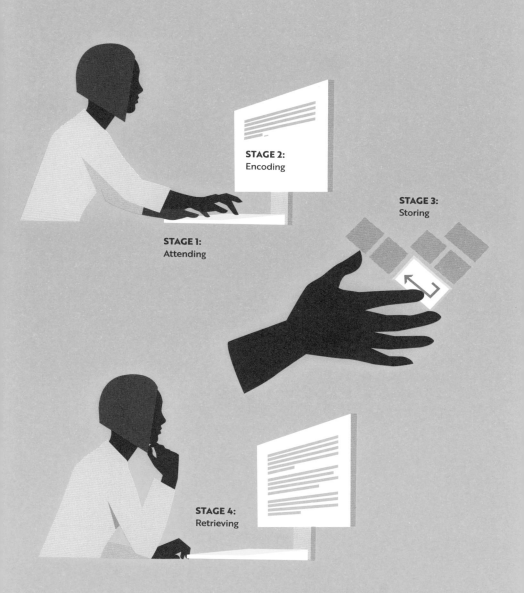

STAGE 1:
Attending

STAGE 2:
Encoding

STAGE 3:
Storing

STAGE 4:
Retrieving

Miller's information processing theory was inspired by computers. To understand this, imagine you are writing an essay on your laptop. The computer attends to the symbols you are typing. They are encoded as they appear on the page. Pressing 'Save' stores the encoded information in a specific location – say, your file folder entitled 'Essays'. You may then have to submit the essay – to do this, you retrieve the file from the Essays folder, where it was stored, and send it along. Like computers, we too have processes for encoding, saving and retrieving information.

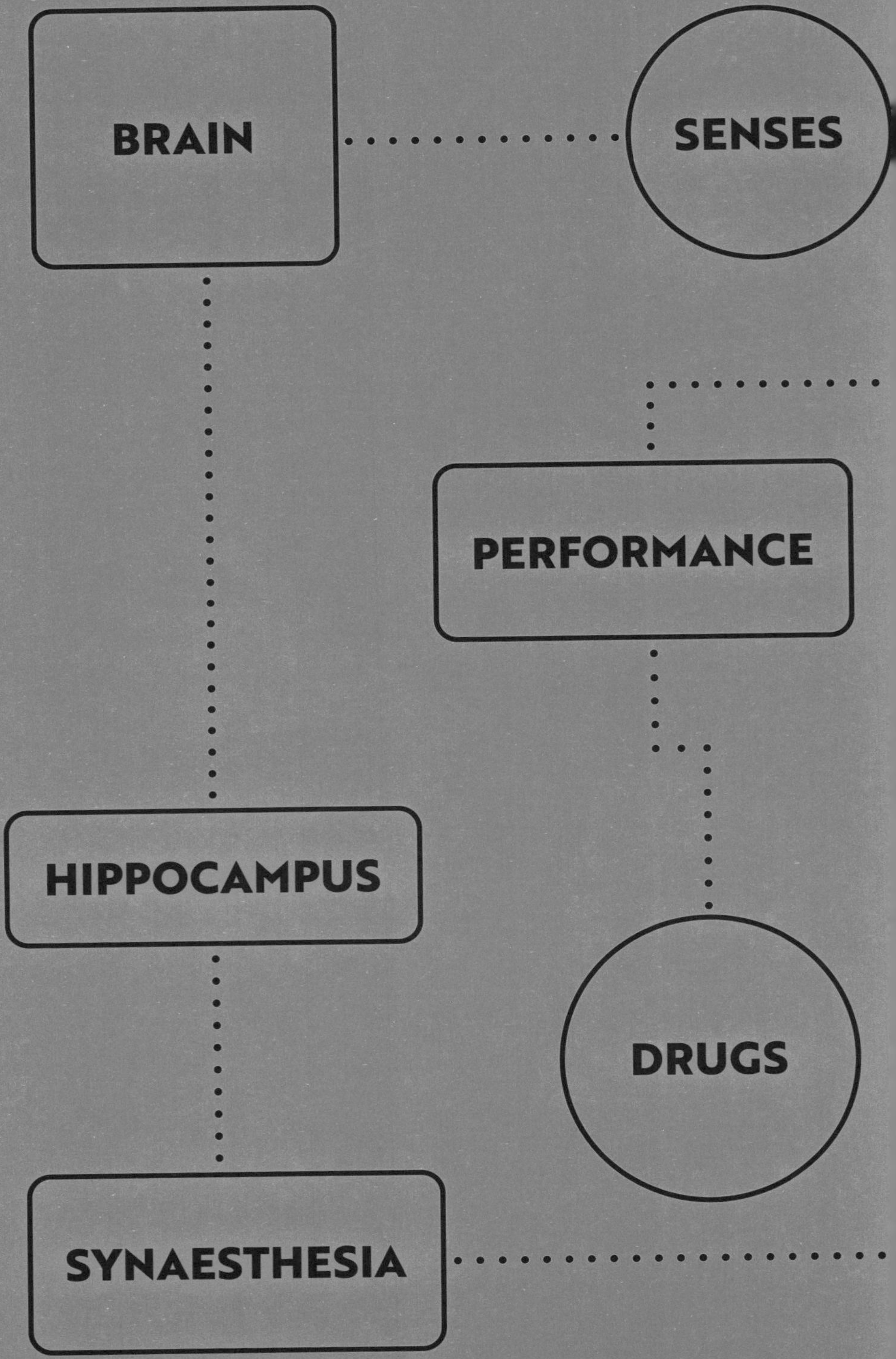
BRAIN
SENSES
PERFORMANCE
HIPPOCAMPUS
DRUGS
SYNAESTHESIA

CHAPTER 4

BIOLOGICAL PSYCHOLOGY

FEELINGS

EQUILIBRIOCEPTION

INTRODUCTION

It's rare for discoveries to repeatedly break ground in any discipline, yet biological psychology sees more significant findings than any other branch of psychology. This chapter distils some of the most revolutionary discoveries.

Scientists have revealed we have more than 50 **SENSES**. We have a sense that tells us where our body parts are in space, called proprioception, which enables us to navigate a spoonful of pudding to our mouth with or without our eyes open. We also have ≠, which uses the liquid in the inner ear to help us know which way is up, and whether or not we're revving up or slowing down. We also rely on equally critical internal senses, so we know when we're hungry or if our bladder's full. Senses can interact, and this happens in overdrive in **SYNAESTHESIA**, where there is a permanent blending of senses.

Our senses are key to how we experience and navigate the world, as well as how we feel. But emotions are more than just sensations in our body. They emerge as a result of how we respond to the information our senses give us, our behaviours, thoughts and how we interpret the world. Psychologists know that changing any one of these elements changes how we feel, as can increasing the stress in our lives. The **YERKES-DODSON LAW** explains how to win with stress, and is linked to findings that we're sharper with increases in mental or physiological pressure – but only to a point. Too much and we risk drops in mental and physical well-being, where we're at risk of bad habits such as relying on coffee to keep going.

Biological psychology has uncovered how drugs such as caffeine, prescribed medications such as antidepressants, and recreational drugs such as marijuana work. They interact with receptors and alter **NEUROTRANSMITTERS** in the brain. Depression drugs help the brain to recycle serotonin, one of 50 neurotransmitters scientists have discovered.

When our brains let us down, such as failing to recognise a familiar face, we may wish we could blame a drug, although it's only a problem if it is happening continually, as with the disorder **PROSOPAGNOSIA**, or face blindness, which arises from damage to the **FUSIFORM GYRUS**. By studying monkeys, scientists have pinpointed six areas in the brain responsible for facial recognition, called **FACE PATCHES**. Some cells detect distances between our eyes; others respond to textures in skin.

One of the most exciting findings within biological psychology has been that we can strengthen the memory centre of the brain, and actually make it grow larger and work better with training. That's what Maguire discovered: the iconic London taxi drivers beef up their **HIPPOCAMPUS** by learning the myriad, complex routes around London.

BIOLOGICAL PSYCHOLOGY MAP

AFFECT
Our experience of feeling, emotion or mood. It contributes to a range of mental states, not just emotion, and can influence how we interpret stimuli.

SENSES
We have more than 50 internal and external senses, which are key to how we experience and navigate the world, as well as how we feel.

APPRAISALS
Our interpretations, which play a key role in emotion, can be causal, when our thoughts relating to a stimulus make us feel a certain way.

PHYSIOLOGICAL RESPONSE
Changes in the body that are integral to our emotional experience, and which include processes in the nerves and/or nervous system.

FACE PATCHES
Six different areas of the macaque brain that contain face-selective neurons, which respond to differences in face shape or appearance (Tsao and Chang).

FIGHT OR FLIGHT
Bodily response to a potentially stressful situation: adrenalin surges, breathing and pulse rate quicken; prepares individuals to fight or flee to safety.

YERKES-DODSON LAW
Performance increases with physiological or mental arousal, but when arousal levels are too high, performance then declines.

RESPONSES

AROUSAI

PROPRIOCEPTION

SYNAESTHESIA
Permanent blending of the senses; occurs when the stimulation of one sense triggers a second, different sense.

SYNAPSES
Small gaps between neurons or between a neuron and a muscle or gland, where nerve impulses are relayed, usually by a neurotransmitter.

HIPPOCAMPUS
A seahorse-shaped structure in the brain's temporal lobe; key to memory and learning but also involved in emotion and motivation.

FUSIFORM GYRUS
Key brain area towards the base of the skull, involved in face recognition and colour perception.

NEUROTRANSMITTERS
Chemical messengers that allow neurons to communicate with other neurons, or with glands or muscles, via a synapse; they bind to receptors on the adjacent neuron.

PLACE CELLS
Specialised hippocampal cells that become active when an animal arrives at a particular location (O'Keefe); a key discovery in cognitive mapping.

PROSOPAGNOSIA
Face blindness, which arises from damage to the fusiform gyrus.

WALDEYER'S NEURON THEORY
The theory that the nervous system is made up of discrete brain cells, with gaps in between the cells.

NERVOUS SYSTEMS
Consisting of nerves, glands and organs, the sympathetic nervous system controls the fight or flight response; the parasympathetic prepares the body to rest and digest.

How do you make sense of it all?

→ We hear, taste, smell, see and touch, right? The body has five senses, enshrined in dogma. Only it's not quite that simple. Dig a little deeper, and you'll find that the exact number of senses is up for grabs.

A sense is a biological system that helps us to gather information about the world and respond to change. It's thought that the concept of five basic senses dates back to the time of Aristotle, because his book *On the Soul* contains separate chapters for vision, hearing, touch, smell and taste. Today, however, we realise that this is overly simplistic.

Close your eyes and touch your nose with your index finger. This feat is possible because of another bodily sense, proprioception, which gives us an awareness of where our body parts are in space. It's made possible by specialised receptors inside the muscles that tell the brain what is going on. Equilibrioception is another sense. It involves the fluid-filled system in the inner ear and helps us to determine gravity and acceleration, so we know which way is up and whether we are speeding up or slowing down. Along with the classic five, these are all examples of external senses.

We have numerous internal senses, too, which detect and respond to changes from inside our bodies. Hunger and thirst are the most obvious examples, but we can also sense pain, as well as when we need to go to the toilet. At a subconscious level, we monitor and sense many other internal signals, such as the beating of the heart, breathing and blood pressure. When all these are taken into account, scientists now think there could be more than 50 different senses.

The senses can interact with and influence one another, too. The colour and texture of food, for example, can often affect its taste. Some people experience a permanent blending of the senses. This is called synaesthesia, and it comes in many forms. For example, a person may taste sounds or hear colours. Around 5 per cent of people experience synaesthesia, but because the experience is so personal, it often goes unreported. Many synaesthetes simply presume this is how everyone experiences the world around them.

MIRROR-TOUCH SYNAESTHESIA

Synaesthesia occurs when the stimulation of one sense triggers a second, different sense. There are many different types. Some people hear words as colours, or music as shapes. One of the strangest varieties is mirror-touch synaesthesia, where a person feels the sensation of being touched when they see someone else being touched. If they see someone being tapped on the shoulder, for example, it feels as though they themselves are being tapped in the same place.

How are you feeling?

→ How we create then experience a feeling is linked to our physical sensations and our responses to them, our behaviours as well as thoughts, and the meaning we give them. Changing one of these elements can change how we feel.

Changes in the body, or our physiological response, are integral to our emotional experience, and include breathing, heart rate and neurochemical activity (processes in the nerves and/or nervous system). William James (1884) suggested that we feel frightened because of our physiological response; others argue that basic emotions provoke a specific bodily response, with variations across individuals and cultures.

Appraisals, or our interpretations, play a key role in emotion. If we see a snake and interpret it as threatening, a physiological response and experience of fear follows. In this instance, the appraisal of the stimulus, or snake, is causal; that is, our thoughts relating to the snake make us feel a certain way. Our physiological responses and how we appraise them can depend on the context within which we are experiencing them. For instance, a racing heart and sweaty palms could be appraised as anxiety in an exam situation, or as excitement on a roller-coaster.

When it comes to emotions, these are understood to be a combination of stimuli, bodily states and affect. Affect describes our experience of feeling, emotion or mood. It contributes to a range of mental states, not just emotion. Are tears and pangs of tension in our belly a sign of sadness, or hunger as we chop an onion for dinner? Affect can also influence how we interpret stimuli. For instance, we might perceive a facial expression differently depending on how we feel or our own interpretation biases. Someone with a negative interpretation bias might see an ambiguous gesture such as a smile as a sign of being laughed at rather than a sign of friendliness.

These theories give us clues about how to change our emotional experiences by changing how we think, our behaviours or how our bodies feel. When we fall in love, we see feelings of panic and nervousness as signs of excitement. Might we learn to see panic in other situations as excitedness rather than fear, and thereby calm our nerves?

INTERPRETATION BIAS

In this scenario, the person holding the snake interprets the situation as safe and therefore feels at ease. The person looking at her holding the snake interprets the situation as threatening and experiences fear as a result.

Do you work better under pressure?

⟶ **Stress can lead to sweaty palms and shallow breathing. No one likes to feel overwhelmed at work, but studies show that a little bit of stress can sometimes improve performance.**

Be it taking an exam or speaking in public, stressful situations can trigger a series of unpleasant changes in the body. Adrenalin levels surge, the pulse rate quickens and breaths come thick and fast. This is known as the fight or flight response because it prepares individuals to either stand up and fight or flee to safety. An ancient and involuntary survival strategy, it's controlled by a bunch of nerves, glands and organs called the sympathetic nervous system. The parasympathetic nervous system, in contrast, has a calming effect. Breaths become slower and the heart rate declines. It prepares the body to rest and digest. The two antagonistic systems represent opposite ends of the arousal spectrum, but which is better for you?

Research has shown that when it comes to performance, a little stress can actually be beneficial. In a 1908 study, Robert Yerkes and John Dodson found that mice were better at learning a task when they received a 'moderate' electric shock, and worse at learning the task when they received a 'mild' or 'extreme' shock. It led the psychologists to formulate the Yerkes-Dodson law. This states that performance increases with physiological or mental arousal, but only to a point. When arousal levels are too high, performance then declines. It's good, for example, to have a few nerves before standing up to speak in public, but not so many that you forget your lines. Added to this, the optimal arousal level depends on the complexity and familiarity of the task. It's more than possible to hoover the living room while listening to a scary audiobook, but you wouldn't want a surgeon similarly distracted.

The law remains popular despite many scientists criticising the design of the 1908 study, and it has since been applied to many areas of human performance, including the workplace. Here, critics caution that the law has been used to 'legitimise' the practice of increasing work stress levels, when newer research has confirmed the link between stress and deteriorating physical and mental health.

STRESS AND PERFORMANCE

According to the Yerkes-Dodson law, a moderate amount of stress can be beneficial for performance. You can't perform if you're so laid back that you're asleep, but nor can you perform when you're so stressed out that you can't think straight. There is an optimum level of stress, somewhere in the middle between alertness and anxiety, which can help us to sharpen our focus and game.

How do drugs blow your mind?

⟶ Fortunately, there is no drug that can literally 'blow' your mind, but many can alter the way that it works. From sharpening your concentration to giving you the munchies, many drugs alter the delicate balance of chemicals that exists inside your brain.

In the late 19th century, Spanish neuroscientist Santiago Ramón y Cajal looked down a microscope and drew what he saw. The result was hundreds of beautiful images of brain cells. His experiments showed that there were gaps between these cells, prompting Heinrich Waldeyer to formulate his neuron theory. This states that the nervous system is made up of discrete brain cells, and today we still concur. The brain and spinal cord are indeed made up of billions of these neurons, which are separated from one another by small gaps called synapses.

Neurons communicate with one another and relay information around the body. The information travels along the neuron in electrical form, but when it reaches a synapse, it has to be converted into a chemical form so it can cross the gap and carry on its way. These chemicals are known as neurotransmitters, and they bind to specialised proteins on the adjacent neuron called receptors. Some neurotransmitters, such as adrenalin and glutamate, go on to increase neuronal activity. These are called excitatory neurotransmitters. Others, such as adenosine and serotonin, slow down neuronal activity. These are referred to as inhibitory. More than 50 different neurotransmitters are known.

Mind-altering drugs work because they interact with these receptors, and alter the balance of neurotransmitters in the brain. They can be everyday substances such as caffeine, prescribed medications such as antidepressants, or recreational drugs such as marijuana.

Caffeine binds to and blocks the activity of adenosine receptors, effectively causing levels of adenosine to drop. Rising levels of adenosine usually make people feel sleepy, so caffeine counteracts this, giving you that perky, wide-awake feeling. It also causes the brain's blood vessels to constrict, which is why you may get a headache. Antidepressants bind to serotonin receptors and temporarily increase the availability of serotonin, while the active component of marijuana – tetrahydrocannabinol (THC) – binds to the brain's cannabinoid receptors to produce a calming effect and elevated levels of dopamine.

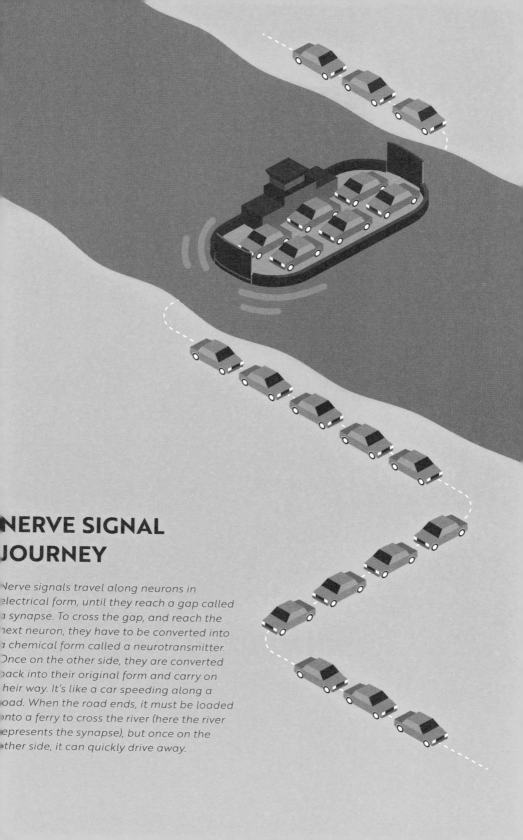

NERVE SIGNAL JOURNEY

Nerve signals travel along neurons in electrical form, until they reach a gap called a synapse. To cross the gap, and reach the next neuron, they have to be converted into a chemical form called a neurotransmitter. Once on the other side, they are converted back into their original form and carry on their way. It's like a car speeding along a road. When the road ends, it must be loaded onto a ferry to cross the river (here the river represents the synapse), but once on the other side, it can quickly drive away.

How do we know anyone?

→ We recognise people mostly from their faces. Key brain cells respond to specific facial features, helping us to recognise not just any old mug, but the faces of ourselves and everyone we know.

From waving to your neighbour to grimacing at your boss, the ability to recognise someone else's face is an important skill to have. It's an asset that most of us acquire early in life, and apart from the odd social gaff, we carry it well into old age. It helps us to determine not only who someone is, but also what they are feeling and thinking, making facial recognition an important part of social interaction.

Scientists have learned a lot about how we recognise faces from studying people who have lost the ability, through brain injury or illness. Famously, the neurologist Oliver Sacks described 'the man who mistook his wife for a hat'. A patient of Sacks', the man suffered from visual agnosia, a rare condition that robbed him of the ability to recognise familiar objects and people by sight. Similarly, people with prosopagnosia, or face blindness, are unable to recognise familiar faces, including their own. Often, there is damage to the fusiform gyrus, a key brain area towards the base of the skull that seems primed to respond to faces.

Imaging studies, where healthy people look at faces while lying in a scanner, have since confirmed the importance of this region in the brain, but studies in primates have gone even further, pinpointing some of the individual cells that are responsible. The adult macaque brain contains billions of neurons, but recognising a face may involve as few as 200. Research by Doris Tsao and Steven Le Chang showed that these cells are located in six different areas or face patches. Some of them fire in response to differences in shape, such as the space between the eyes or the width of the mouth, while others respond to differences in appearance, such as skin tone and texture.

Macaque and human brains are very similar, so extrapolating from this, it appears that our brains process faces as the sum of separate subtle parts, and not as a single entity. So, if you 'accidentally ignore' your boss in the corridor, you can blame it on your neurons.

MR VEGETABLE FACE

What do you see? For most of us, the answer is obvious. It's a man whose face is made of vegetables. For the estimated 2 per cent of people who suffer from face blindness, however, there is no face; it's just the raw ingredients for a vegetable curry. Face blindness can run in families, or more rarely, be acquired through brain injury or disease. People often deal with the issue by using non-facial cues to recognise people, such as their clothes or voice.

How does a taxi driver remember a short cut?

→ Two words: the Knowledge. The time and effort taken by cabbies to memorise London's labyrinthine street map causes part of their brain to grow, with spectacular navigational results.

The meter is running as the cabbie takes a sharp left. He assures you it's the quickest route, but before you're able to protest, you're there. Tip the taxi driver, and thank 'the Knowledge'.

The Knowledge is London's legendary taxi-driver test. Before they take to the streets, cabbies have to memorise the layout of 25,000 roads and thousands of places of interest. They have to pass numerous exams across several years, and when they're done they know all the back routes and side roads without ever needing to fire up the sat nav. So how do they do it?

Scientists suspected involvement of the hippocampus, a seahorse-shaped structure in the brain's temporal lobe. Fifty years ago, John O'Keefe proved the existence of place cells: specialised hippocampal cells that become active when an animal arrives at a particular location. His discovery helped launch the idea of cognitive maps, which are the mental representations that we make of places and routes.

Studies have shown that species that cache a lot of food tend to have bigger hippocampi than similarly sized species that don't have to remember detailed spatial information, prompting Eleanor Maguire to wonder if the idea might hold true for taxi drivers. In a 2000 study, she used MRI scans to compare the brains of cabbies and non-cabby controls, and found that taxi drivers do indeed have larger hippocampi.

The study suggested a link between spatial memory and hippocampal size, but it didn't prove that learning the Knowledge causes the change. Maybe people with bigger hippocampi are just more likely to become cabbies.

So, Maguire scanned the brains of novice cabbies before and after they completed their training, and compared the scans with their test scores. Before the Knowledge, the drivers all had similarly sized hippocampi, but after training, the brain structure was larger in those who had passed their test. Put simply, learning the Knowledge does make your brain bigger, and this seems to be why London taxi drivers make short shrift of shortcuts.

THE KNOWLEDGE

Learning the layout of London's streets – aka 'the Knowledge' – causes the brains of taxi drivers to change. A key structure involved in learning and memory, the hippocampus, gets bigger. The same cannot be said for doctors, who also have to learn a lot of information, or memory champions, who have to learn a lot of lists. Instead, the change is a response to learning navigational information, as the brain builds up a detailed cognitive map of its local environment.

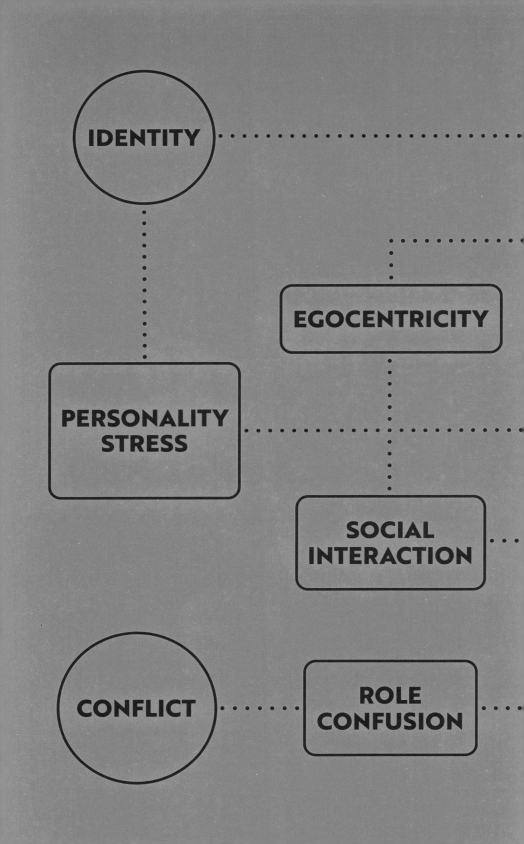

CHAPTER 5

DEVELOPMENTAL PSYCHOLOGY

ATTACHMENTS

PSYCHOSOCIAL DEVELOPMENT

INTRODUCTION

I magine in two years being leaner, taller, more capable and curious than you already are. It's difficult to contemplate that you'd change much over two years. Yet, in the distant past, you did, and many times over. At no other time in our lives do we develop as rapidly as when we're children. This chapter is devoted to the fascinating facts about how children learn and grow, and the most important stages of development they seemingly breeze through.

Bowlby famously spotted that our early relationships must dish out more than food for us to survive and thrive. Comfort, protection and security are key ingredients for creating lifelong, healthy bonds. **MARY AINSWORTH** studied how children connect to their mothers and why it's important. By watching how children react when their mother and a stranger enter and leave a room, she devised core categories of attachment style, from secure to insecure. The latter seems to be linked to problems with relationships, self-esteem and mental health in later life. But does it make it harder to deal with stress?

Before we could check how people cope, psychologists had to determine how to assess stress. Around the same time that attachment theory was gaining traction, Holmes and Rahe got to grips measuring the nitty gritty of big events, such as moving house, bereavement and divorce. Although these can link to later ill health, Kanner discovered that our **DAILY HASSLES** were far more problematic than a period of time punctuated by intense **LIFE EVENTS**. Since then, psychologists have discovered that an insecure attachment style hampers how people deal with crippling pressure. The early experiences that form this style can make reaching out for help an uncomfortable strategy.

Whatever bond children share with caregivers, they're only able to see the world from their own point of view. On their route to adulthood, they evolve through Piaget's stages of cognitive development and grapple with **THEORY OF MIND**. By adolescence, they grasp that other people experience different thoughts and feelings to their own, and can even infer what they might be.

Erikson's theory of psychosocial development spans our whole life. As babies, we learn about trust and mistrust, with themes of hope, and by 65 we're focussed on acceptance versus despair, with themes of wisdom.

There is meaning in almost everything a child does, right down to why they play. Playing helps children to learn to give and take, and to communicate. By five years old, they're able to co-operate when they play, which is hugely important for honing the capacity to collaborate and essential for our success as a species.

DEVELOPMENTAL PSYCHOLOGY MAP

AUTISM
Lifelong developmental disability that affects how people communicate and interact with the world; deficits in theory of mind are common.

COLLABORATION
Assigning and accepting the distinct roles that each person plays in working towards a common goal.

JUDITH DUNN
British psychologist and academic (1939–) specialising in social developmental psychology and the nature of young children's social understanding.

THEORY OF MIND
Ability to infer the beliefs, emotions, perspectives and thoughts of other people, which we use in everyday social situations.

SOCIAL RELATIONSHIPS
Connections and bonds made with others outside of the home, through which children learn how to play in a 'socially acceptable' way.

FALSE BELIEFS
Misconceptions resulting from incorrect reasoning or assumptions; an important aspect of theory of mind.

EGOCENTRICITY
Perceiving the world only from our own point of view and thinking that others see the world as we do.

DAILY HASSLES
The everyday strains we experience; Kanner's scale (1981) focusses on 117 of these as predictors of stress-related illness.

SOCIAL READJUSTMENT RATING SCALE (SRRS)
The Holmes and Rahe Stress Scale (1967) is a self-assessment tool for stress measurement, which works by valuing life events with 'life change units'.

LIFE EVENTS
Significant stressful experiences that we encounter across our lives. Holmes and Rahe included 43 in their stress-quantifying questionnaire (1967) and assigned relative values.

STRESS

DYNAMICS

PLAYFUL DISRUPTION
Testing the limits of certain social situations through externalising behaviour.

BOWLBY'S ATTACHMENT THEORY
The bond that we develop with caregivers; early relationships are key, not just for a supply of food, but also for comfort, protection and nurturing.

REPRESENTATIONS
Modes of thinking that help us to learn, from enactive representation at the start of life, through iconic representation, to symbolic representation (Bruner).

MARY AINSWORTH
American-Canadian psychologist (1913–99) who observed three attachment styles in children aged 9–18 months – secure, insecure–avoidant and insecure–ambivalent, in 'The Strange Situation Task'.

VIRTUES
Eight desirable traits that can be acquired at each of the eight stages of life: hope, will, purpose, competency, fidelity, love, care and wisdom (Erikson).

PSYCHOSOCIAL CONFLICTS
Incompatibility between our psychological needs and the surrounding social environment. Their resolution, or otherwise, impacts on our personality development (Erikson).

SENSE OF SELF
A sense of direction in life, commitment to our own beliefs and awareness of our role in society.

LIFE STAGES

Can stress sink a sailor?

⟶ **Prolonged stress can 'sink' just about anyone, sailors included, but stress comes in many forms. Psychologists have devised a variety of rating scales to quantify the quantity and potential consequences of the stresses we experience.**

Life is a bumpy road beset with challenges and change. Some changes, such as the birth of a baby or being in an accident, can be stressful, but how much stress do we experience and what are the repercussions?

In 1967, psychiatrists Thomas Holmes and Richard Rahe designed a questionnaire to quantify stress. It focusses on life events, which are the significant stressful experiences that we encounter across our lives. They assigned values to 43 life events according to their potential impact. The death of a spouse scores highest, with 100 'life change units', and divorces come second, with 73. Lesser life events, such as starting a new school, going on holiday or receiving a parking ticket, score twenty or less. They called it the Social Readjustment Rating Scale (SRRS).

Three years later, Rahe tested his questionnaire on 2,500 American sailors. He found a positive correlation between their scores and subsequent ill health. As the number and severity of life events ramped up, so too did the frequency of illness. Stress, it seems, really can sink a sailor.

The American Institute of Stress now predicts that an annual score of over 300 life change units means a person has an 80 per cent chance of developing a stress-related illness, such as anxiety or depression, in the next two years. Lower scores come with lower risks, but while there is good evidence to suggest that chronic stress can contribute to ill health, there is less evidence to support the ranking of stressful life events in this way.

For one thing, most people don't suffer major life events often, so a better measure of stress might focus on the everyday strains we experience, such as worrying about our weight or losing our phone. With this in mind, A.D. Kanner devised another scale, in 1981, which focusses on 117 of these so-called daily hassles. Hassles, he found, are a better predictor of stress-related illness than the SRRS. Multiple minor stresses can sink a sailor too.

LIFE EVENTS

Losing a loved one or being sent to jail are obviously stressful, but so-called 'happy' events can be major sources of stress too. Holmes and Rahe included both positive and negative life events in their Social Readjustment Rating Scale. Pregnancy and going on holiday, for example, can be both positive and stressful. The scale reveals how the effects of stress can be cumulative, and how multiple smaller life events can have just as much impact as a lesser number of large ones.

1. Death of a spouse
2. Going to jail
3. Pregnancy
4. Starting school
5. Going on holiday

1
2
3
4
5

100   63   40   26   13

LIFE CHANGE UNITS

Should you download a strange attachment?

→ Nope. You should download a secure one. Whether emailing or developing relationships, secure attachments are better. For children, early attachments with their caregivers have long-lasting effects. Secure ones are thought to improve well-being in later life.

An attachment in psychological terms is not something that we can just download from others. According to attachment theory, it represents the emotional and physical bond that we develop with our caregivers. It builds over time and depends on how and when we are responded to by our caregivers as well as their own attachment styles.

Attachment theory was developed in the 1950s by John Bowlby. He investigated the mother–infant relationship in monkeys and showed the importance of early relationships, not just for a supply of food, but also for comfort, protection and nurturing.

Mary Ainsworth expanded on Bowlby's theories in the 1970s and came up with three different attachment styles in children aged nine to eighteen months: secure, insecure–avoidant and insecure–ambivalent. To assess a child's attachment style, Ainsworth looked at how they reacted to their mother and a stranger entering and leaving the room in 'The Strange Situation Task'. A fourth attachment style of 'disorganised' was added later to account for children who did not seem to fit in anywhere else.

Although very popular and supported by many studies, attachment theory has received criticism for its lack of cultural universality. Keller (2018) highlights that the theory is based on the typical Western, middle-class nuclear family structure, in which a child has one main caregiver and emotions are responded to and encouraged in a certain way. Obviously, this is not how the whole world raises children – some cultures use community-based parenting strategies and respond to emotions differently.

What do attachment styles mean for us? Research suggests that early attachment styles can impact us in later life. Insecure attachments have been linked to low self-esteem, difficulties in relationships and increased risk of receiving a mental health diagnosis. In adults, attachment theory can be used to understand a person's life experiences as well as inform assessments and treatments for mental health difficulties. Adult attachment styles can be measured with the 'Adult Attachment Interview' and classified as dismissing, autonomous, preoccupied or unresolved.

THE FOUR ATTACHMENT STYLES

The four attachment styles in children as observed in Ainsworth's The Strange Situation Task. The experiment helped psychologist Mary Ainsworth observe *then categorise children's attachment styles. However, the experiment was limited to a Western, middle-class nuclear family set-up.*

SECURE
Distressed when caregiver leaves.
Avoidant of stranger when alone but friendly when caregiver present.
Positive when caregiver returns.
Caregiver can comfort child.

INSECURE–AMBIVALENT
Highly distressed when caregiver leaves.
Avoids and fears stranger.
Seeks caregiver but resists contact.
Difficult to comfort.

INSECURE–AVOIDANT
Not distressed when caregiver leaves.
Not distressed at stranger and plays normally.
Shows little interest when caregiver returns.
Caregiver and stranger equally able to comfort child.

DISORGANISED
Fearful or apprehensive about approaching caregiver.
Appears confused or disoriented.
Conflicting behaviour, e.g. anger followed by being in a daze.

How's your child's ego?

➝ It might seem rather big when they're young, as toddlers can only see the world from their viewpoint. But they quickly evolve through four key milestones. By adolescence, they will have grasped that other people experience different thoughts and feelings.

In 1936, Swiss psychologist Piaget suggested that every child between the ages of 0 and 11+ progresses through four predefined stages of cognitive development. Throughout these stages, children are actively learning about and exploring their environment, developing their mental representations and knowledge (schemas – see page 62) about the world. According to Piaget, during this time, a child's egocentricity reduces.

So, what is egocentricity? It's the tendency to perceive the world only from our own point of view and assume that others see the world as we do. So, children are selfish? Maybe, but they're a work in progress!

The first step in the reduction of egocentricity is the sensorimotor stage (0–2 years). A child is combining their senses and motor skills to build intelligence. They start learning that objects exist and events occur even when out of their own sight (object permanence).

Then comes the preoperational stage (2–7 years). Children are exploring through symbolic, or pretend, play. They tend to focus on only one aspect of a situation at one time (centration) and they are still pretty absorbed in their own visual world. They might use speech in their play but this would be to externalise their own thinking rather than to communicate with others.

Stage 3, the concrete operational stage (7–11 years), marks the beginning of logical thought and rules, and applying them to physical objects. Children start to understand that their thoughts and feelings are unique and that other people have their own, but they might not yet be able to think about how or what the other person is experiencing.

The final stage, the formal operational stage (11+ years), involves applying that logical thought to abstract problems (abstract thinking). The ability to think hypothetically helps children comprehend different points of view to their own.

Do we stop there? Piaget's theory did, but many people believe that we continue to develop our schema well into our twenties and build on what we know through interactions with others and, importantly, our social environment.

THE THREE MOUNTAINS TASK

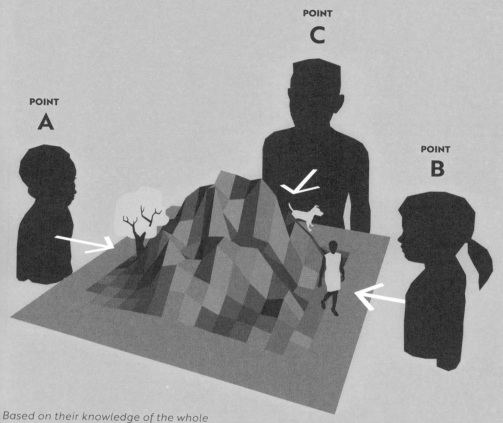

POINT A

POINT C

POINT B

Based on their knowledge of the whole scene, can the child grasp what someone sitting at point C is currently seeing? A four-year-old child can only comprehend what is in their own current view (point A); at age seven they have a more objective perspective (point B); but it is not until age eleven (Piaget's formal operational stage) when they can correctly identify a different viewpoint to their own (point C). It's as if each stage is a building block for constructing a less egocentric world view.

Why does a baby shake a rattle?

→ Cognitive development is all about moving from the concrete to the abstract; from rattles to imaginary games. We progress from knowledge based on actions to knowledge based on images or symbols.

Jerome Bruner was interested in how humans construct, represent and organise knowledge, and how different modes of thinking, or representations, help us to develop our learning.

Enactive representation is used in the first year of life, and so relates directly to why a baby shakes a rattle. Our thinking is based on physical actions: we learn by doing rather than by reasoning. Babies use their motor skills to shake a rattle, while activating multiple senses, such as hearing the rattle and watching it move. As well as providing stimulation and amusement, the rattle signifies the ability to learn and retain knowledge. Babies learn that doing this action results in certain outcomes, and they will develop muscle memory, so that when they pick up the rattle again they know what to do with it. This type of action-based representation is also used later in life when, for example, we learn to ride a bike.

Between one and six years old, we start to use iconic representations – experiencing concepts through visual images. This is not always conscious storage, but it can help us to digest new information, such as an image of a pizza to demonstrate fractions.

Storing knowledge based on fixed actions or images (enactive and iconic representations) can be restrictive, as it might be difficult to use what you know in a different context. Symbolic representations – information stored in the form of a code or symbol, such as language – are more flexible and can be manipulated. For example, we learn that a dog is a certain class of animal, or understand that a plus sign (+) means to add two things together. The development of symbolic thinking starts at around age seven, and is key to our overall cognitive development.

So how does this translate to education? Unlike Piaget (see page 62), Bruner believed that any subject can be taught to a child of any age. The key is how you structure the information to fit the form of representation the child's knowledge is currently organised by – starting with simplified ideas and building up to be more complex.

BRUNER'S SCAFFOLDING

In 1983, Bruner and colleagues coined the term 'scaffolding' to describe how teachers and parents may provide a framework (a scaffold, see below) to assist children in their learning. The aim is that children will be able to eventually master problems by themselves. How can it be done? By modelling an action, such as shaking a rattle, so that the behaviour can be imitated, giving clues for solving a problem, or by restructuring the problem into parts like scaffolding that can be built upon.

Is social interaction child's play?

→ **Yes, says Judith Dunn, a psychologist and academic specialising in social developmental psychology. Dunn's research explores how young children learn to interact in socially appropriate ways.**

Children grow up in a complex social world. In every family structure there are roles and rules that the child has to model and learn, and it is this that helps them to develop socially: their social play, co-operation and teasing. The quality of family interaction, and whether a child can discuss as well as reflect on their experiences, influences their understanding of social norms and emotions. Dunn found that children as young as four were capable of recalling their own and referring to others' emotions and reasoning when talking about their experience of starting day care, for example: 'He was sad because he wanted his mum.'

A child's experiences outside of the home, such as in preschool, are also important. By three or four years old, children have increased independence from adults. They have more opportunity for social relationships with other children, through which they learn how to give and take in order to play in a socially acceptable way. There is less of a power dynamic in this interaction, and so children are more likely to share their thoughts and feelings with friends, and as a result, learn more about others.

With better communication comes greater ability to collaborate – to assign and accept the distinct roles that each person plays in working towards a common goal. Dunn found that by the ages of four and five, children engage in co-operative play, such as building a snowman together. These skills are also beneficial later on in life when collaborating at school and in other typical social settings, such as playing sports.

When we know someone well enough, we have an understanding of what might upset or annoy them, and therefore how to tease them. Dunn suggests that this (unsurprisingly) starts with our siblings. Playful disruption, such as stealing your sister's Nintendo, is a way of attracting attention and having a laugh, but also of testing the limits of certain social situations. With an adult's (such as a parent's or teacher's) input, we develop an understanding of what is socially 'right' and 'wrong'.

FAMILIES, HOMES, INTERACTIONS

Dunn's early work was based on observing sibling relationships in the family home. This included observing interesting family dynamics around the dinner table. Children as young as two showed a clear practical grasp of how to annoy and/or comfort their siblings. Due to the influence of the family and environment on a child's understanding and ability to interact socially, there is potential for considerable individual differences.

Are children mind readers?

→ As adults, we can take a guess at what is going on in other people's minds and how this might differ from our own. But we aren't born this way! By around five years old, most of us have developed this ability.

Theory of mind is the ability to infer the beliefs, emotions, perspectives and thoughts of other people. But why is it only a theory? We can never know for certain what another person is thinking or why they do something, but we are able to make a guess, or generate a theory, about what is going on in their mind. Without theory of mind, we would assume that everyone has the same thoughts, perspectives and knowledge as we do.

We use theory of mind every day, especially in social situations. For example, imagine it's 7pm, and you and a friend are out for drinks; you feel energetic, but they keep yawning and are struggling to keep their eyes open. You use theory of mind to consider their feelings, and think: 'They look tired; maybe they want to go home.' You ask them this, but they say they are fine. You use theory of mind again to question whether this is how they really feel. Without theory of mind, you would assume that your friend feels as energetic as you do, and you would find it hard to understand why they would say they were fine if they didn't mean it. This is how people with autism can feel; deficits in theory of mind are common in autism and can be spotted during a child's development.

Research suggests there are five main areas of development that lead to a theory of mind in children. These include understanding that people have different desires and beliefs about things, that people can hold false beliefs, and that people can hide their emotions. These areas start to develop at around three years old, though the order in which they develop varies across cultures. Each area forms an important part of a child's theory of mind, and in typical development, this is present by five years old.

The most common task that psychologists use to investigate a child's development of theory of mind tests whether they can understand false beliefs.

THE FALSE-BELIEF TASK

This scenario is described to children to see whether they can understand false beliefs, an important aspect of theory of mind. If they can, they will say that Sally will look for the ball where she left it. If they cannot understand false beliefs, they will assume that Sally knows what they know, and say that she will look in the cupboard.

Sally puts the ball in box.

Sally walks away.

Ann moves the ball to the cupboard.

Where will Sally look?

If all the world's a stage, what's your role?

━━▶ In Erikson's stage theory of psychosocial development, life is a journey from hope through to wisdom, and all virtues in between. It is all about how we navigate our own identity and personality development.

Erikson was interested in identity development from infancy through to adulthood (he coined the term identity crisis). In the 1950s, he proposed eight pre-determined stages of development and eight basic virtues that can be acquired at each stage: hope, will, purpose, competency, fidelity, love, care and wisdom.

Erikson spoke of the psychosocial conflicts – between our own psychological needs and the surrounding social environment – we go through, and their impact on our personality development. Resolution of such conflicts can lead to the development of certain virtues that help us in the future, while unresolved conflicts can lead to vulnerability in later life. For example, if you're unable to develop trust and therefore hope before the age of 2 (e.g. due to a bad caregiver), you might run into challenges in love at age 25. Some conflict is good though – it's literally character building! In the next stage, between ages 2 and 4 (the development of will), while we want some freedom, such as dressing ourselves, we need some rules and protection from our parents.

The adolescent period (age 12–18) is important for establishing a sense of self. As teenagers, we do a lot of experimenting – we've all been through those questionable phases! We are motivated by our peers, wanting to feel accepted in society while also feeling pressure to develop a sense of direction in life. Success in this stage can lead to fidelity – commitment to our own beliefs and sense of self. However, some can be left feeling unsure of themselves or their place in society (role confusion).

If or when we have developed a strong sense of self, in the next stage (age 18–40), we question what we mean to other people. Can we form intimate relationships or do we feel lonely and isolated? In later adulthood (age 40–65) our role flips; we might be nurturing things or children that will continue on after us. Success here would be feeling accomplished and using what we know to help others. Lastly, age 65+, we seek to attain a balance between ego integrity (acceptance) and despair, which hopefully leads to wisdom.

ERIKSON'S VIRTUES

Keeping your age in mind, what role would you be expected to take? A child might be backstage getting into character (hope, will, purpose, age 0–5). A young person might be on stage rehearsing to build confidence (competency, fidelity, age 5–18); or in the stands socialising with other people (love, age 18–40). As we age, we may find ourselves in the wings supporting others (care, age 40–65); or in the audience reflecting on the roles previously played (wisdom, age 65+). However, our environment probably has the biggest role to play in the development of these virtues.

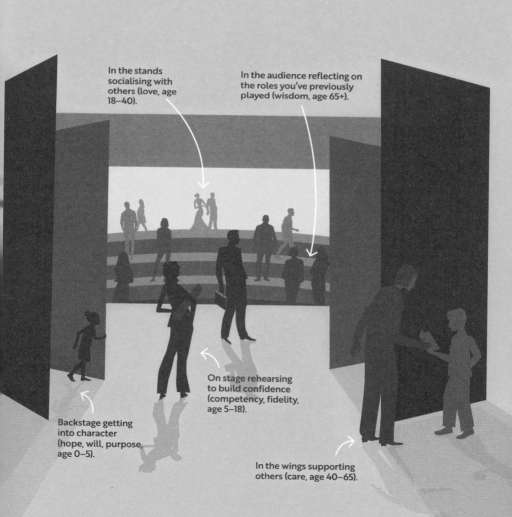

In the stands socialising with others (love, age 18–40).

In the audience reflecting on the roles you've previously played (wisdom, age 65+).

On stage rehearsing to build confidence (competency, fidelity, age 5–18).

Backstage getting into character (hope, will, purpose, age 0–5).

In the wings supporting others (care, age 40–65).

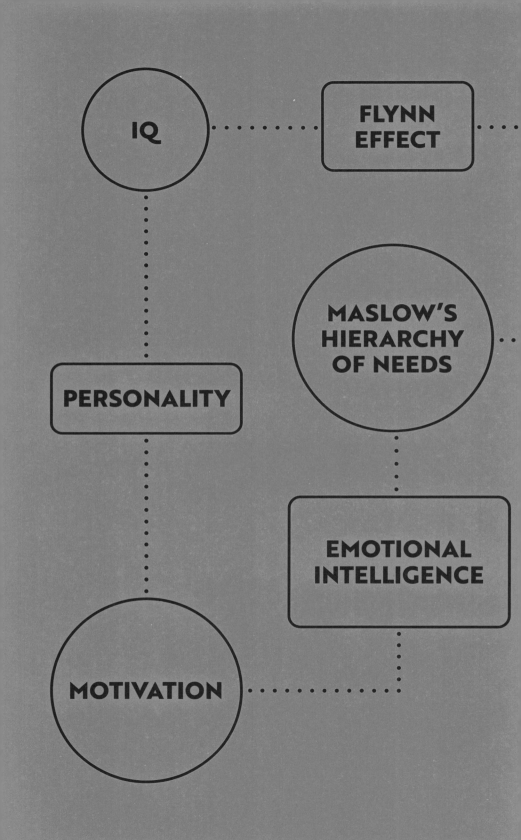

CHAPTER 6

INDIVIDUAL DIFFERENCES

N–ACH

FACTOR ANALYSIS

INTRODUCTION

Some people can achieve anything. We hear about their accomplishments and think they must be more motivated or smarter than us, or perhaps have honed a personality more robust than our own. This chapter is all about our individual differences in the processes intrinsic to our success and satisfaction in the world.

What drives people initially is motivation to meet their basic needs, such as filling an empty stomach and finding warmth from the cold. But once these needs are met, what motivates any one person will link to what's important to them. Most of us are motivated to pursue meaningful needs such as connecting with others; some will be driven to achieve success or experience power. Maslow tells us that the highest motivation is the drive for spiritual centredness, a state of mind that separates the great from the good – and which few people achieve.

Compared to the past, the demands on our brain are varied and complex, and this, in part, explains why we are getting smarter. It's called the **FLYNN EFFECT** and refers to gains seen in intelligence when two periods in history are compared. In Victorian times, for example, the average person would struggle with an intelligence test that someone might ace today.

But psychology is moving away from seeing high performance on a specific test as the standard marker of intelligence. To capture differences between people's skill sets, many psychologists would agree there are multiple – up to eight – types of intelligence, which span linguistic, spatial and existential intelligence. These kinds of intelligence are influenced by education and life experiences, whereas analytical intelligence, measured by IQ tests, is considered to be more innate.

In recent years, **EMOTIONAL INTELLIGENCE (EI)** has emerged as a distinguishing marker of a person's success in the world. Someone who is high in EI can understand how others might feel and adapt their behaviour accordingly. The most successful leaders are thought to be high in EI. Such strong leaders have strong personalities, a core characteristic that distinguishes one person from another, and which is tough to measure. Psychologists have whittled personality measurement down to the **BIG FIVE TRAITS**. Each trait lies on a continuum, so if you are high in the openness trait, it would mean you're inventive and curious, which are at one end, and you'd be less likely to be consistent and cautious, the characteristics sitting at the other end.

Motivation, intelligence and personality certainly differ from person to person and shape how we make sense of the world around us. But the most comprehensive theory to explain individual differences in how people interpret and construct reality is down to Kelly and his construct theory, which posits that we create **CONSTRUCTS** like building blocks that influence our thoughts, behaviours and ultimately our feelings.

INDIVIDUAL DIFFERENCES MAP

FLYNN EFFECT
Gains seen in intelligence
(through average IQ scores)
over time, averaging three IQ
points per decade in many
industrialised societies (Flynn).

ABSTRACT THINKING
Understanding logic and
being able to problem solve;
sometimes referred to as
'fluid IQ'.

MASLOW'S PYRAMID
Structure explaining our
motivations: from the most
basic, survival, at the bottom,
through love and belonging,
to transcendence needs
at the top.

**STERNBERG'S
TRIARCHIC THEORY
OF INTELLIGENCE**
Instead of IQ, there are three
categories of intelligence that
are more relevant in the current
world: practical, creative
and analytical.

**GARDNER'S MULTIPLE
TYPES OF INTELLIGENCE
(MIS)**
Humans have differing
amounts of all the MIs, which
are defined by a strict set of
criteria and fall into
nine types.

INTELLIGENCE

**EMOTIONAL INTELLIGENCE
(EI)**
Consists of five skills that allow
you to maximise your own and
others' performances: self-
awareness, self-regulation,
motivation, empathy, social
skills (Goleman).

DANIEL GOLEMAN
American author and
psychologist (1946–) known
for his work on emotional
intelligence, particularly
how it relates to leadership
and business.

LIMBIC SYSTEM
Part of the brain in the
temporal lobe that controls
our impulses, feelings and
drives. Goleman advised
that business training should
focus on stimulating it.

NEEDS

INTERPRETATION

CONSTRUCTIVE ALTERNATIVISM
Alternative constructs that might help
deal with a situation; understanding
someone else's constructs, to see why
they have acted a certain way (Kelly).

SELF-ACTUALISATION
At the top of Maslow's pyramid:
finding fulfilment and doing
everything within one's
capability. A self-actualised
person is constantly striving
for personal growth.

CONSTRUCTS
Inherently personal mental
templates that help us predict
an outcome, usually based on
our previous experiences (Kelly).
They can influence how we
remember situations.

MCCLELLAND'S 'N-ACH'
'Need for achievement': the
characteristic seen in people
that have the innate desire for
significant accomplishment.

EMERGENT/IMPLICIT POLES
Constructs sit on a scale
between two opposing ends:
the emergent pole, from
where constructs are applied,
and the implicit pole, which
is not actively applied.

**MCCRAE
AND COSTA'S BIG
FIVE TRAITS (OCEAN)**
Five factors that, in
different amounts, can be
used to describe personality
and characterise all adults:
Openness to experience,
Conscientious, Extraversion,
Agreeableness,
Neuroticism.

FACTOR ANALYSIS
Statistical analysis technique that
identifies hidden patterns and shrinks
down huge data sets into a smaller
number of underlying factors.

PERSONALITY

Can humans live by bread alone?

→ Physiologically, yes, but this might not satisfy our emotional needs. According to Maslow, humans are motivated by personal growth and self-discovery. Once the biological need for food is met, we move on to bigger needs.

What motivates us? Maslow advised that our motivations can be organised in a pyramid, with the most basic survival needs, such as food, water and warmth, at the bottom. Once these needs are met, the things that motivate us become more complex, such as the need to be part of a group (love and belongingness), all the way up to the need for values that transcend beyond the personal self, such as the pursuit of religious faith (transcendence needs).

Although these needs are described as a hierarchy, and basic needs must be more or less met before the higher needs, it is thought that people 'skip' around the levels dependent on their personal differences or environment. And once you reach the top, that doesn't mean there is no more motivation. A self-actualised person is constantly striving for personal growth, fulfilled and doing all they are capable of. However, Maslow estimated only 2 per cent of people reach this stage, one of whom was Albert Einstein!

Other psychologists believe humans are motivated differently based on their personalities. For example, David McClelland coined the term 'N-Ach' (from 'need for achievement') to describe the characteristic seen in people who have the innate desire for significant accomplishment. Those high in N-Ach certainly wouldn't be able to live by bread alone; they seek challenges and independence, and the most satisfying reward to them is the recognition of their achievements by others. On the other hand, those who are low in N-Ach aren't motivated by achievement, and might choose easy tasks in order to reduce the chance of failure, or extremely difficult tasks where failure is not as embarrassing. McClelland would give people images of ambiguous social situations and ask them to describe the scenario, in order to determine how much someone is motivated by N-Ach. People could also be classed as motivated by a need for affiliation (N-Aff) or a need for power (N-Pow).

N-ACH

Schultheiss and colleagues found that higher levels of N-Ach (need of achievement) predicted a reduced cortisol response, which is the hormone released when we are stressed, when completing difficult or competitive tasks, such as climbing a mountain. They suggested this might be because those high in N-Ach have learned to associate difficult tasks with the pleasure of overcoming them, leading to a lower stress response than those who haven't.

Are we getting smarter?

→ According to IQ tests, we are getting more intelligent. But these gains in intelligence are not made because we have more basic knowledge; they are made because we have become better at abstract thinking.

It was James Flynn who first studied this rise in IQ in the 1980s, and so the increase of human intelligence scores over time is known as the Flynn effect. Although as a population we have improved in all areas, the biggest gain comes from abstract thinking, which refers to understanding logic and being able to problem solve. It is sometimes referred to as 'fluid IQ'.

We may have become better at these things due to increased access to education, improved health and nutrition, or more exposure to the tests. For example, the popularity of video games helps with spatial reasoning tasks. Being able to manipulate and move objects in the virtual world is good training for an IQ test, where some of the questions involve being able to rotate a shape in your mind. In fact, the average person today would be in the top 2 per cent of scores back in 1910, and the average person from 1910 would score in only the low range today.

Robert Sternberg argues that IQ is not actually that important in the current world. (So don't worry if you don't qualify for Mensa.) Sternberg's theory, the triarchic theory of intelligence, is made up of three subcategories. The first is practical intelligence, which is all about context; it allows us to adapt to new environments and shape the environment we are in. Then there's creative intelligence, the capacity to be flexible and creative. This kind of intelligence is useful when performing tasks that are brand new to you. The final type in this theory is the only one measured by traditional IQ tests: analytical intelligence. This is what allows us to acquire new information and understand and process problems.

Perhaps we need to change the ways we measure intelligence in order to know whether humans really are getting smarter or just getting better at taking tests.

THE SCALE OF CREATIVE INTELLIGENCE

Creative intelligence can be broken down further according to Sternberg. Some people are excellent at handling brand new tasks and finding new ways to problem solve. They might even find ways others wouldn't notice.

Others can perform a task multiple times and then automate it, so it can be done with no extra thought, or even at the same time as other things. Being skilled at one thing doesn't mean you are good at another, however!

How many intelligences are there?

⟶ The traditional definition of intelligence suggests that we are born with one uniform capacity to process things. But psychologists such as Howard Gardner propose that there are in fact up to eight different types of intelligence.

In 1983, Gardner first proposed the idea that humans are not born with the finite amount of intelligence they will ever have. Instead, he said that everyone has differing amounts of all the multiple types of intelligence (MIs). The types of intelligence are defined by a strict set of criteria, and what started as six types is now nine.

The first MI is linguistic: the ability to learn and use language to achieve goals. People high in this include authors, journalists and lawyers. Second is logical-mathematical: a sensitivity to numerical and logical patterns that allows reasoning. Musical is third: if you have the ability to produce and appreciate rhythm, as well as good or even absolute pitch, you might be high in this. The ability to visualise with your mind's eye, being able to judge and manipulate things in the space around you, is known as the spatial MI. Pilots and surgeons are usually high in this. Bodily-kinaesthetic relates to controlling your own body and handling objects skilfully. This also refers to a good sense of timing and capability

to train your own responses – useful if you plan on being a professional athlete. If you can always tell how somebody else is feeling, or always know the right thing to say to calm someone down or cheer them up, you are probably high in interpersonal intelligence: the ability to discern and respond to others' moods. Similar to this, intrapersonal intelligence is all about accessing your own feelings and using that knowledge to guide your own behaviour.

Expertise in recognising and classifying numerous species in one's environment and using this productively is known as naturalistic intelligence. Think Charles Darwin or Jane Goodall. Finally, existential intelligence is the ability to think about and reflect on life's deep questions, such as the meaning of life.

Although Gardner proposed that our unique combination of intelligences is influenced by genetics, MIs must be nurtured and strengthened through personal experience and education. They can also be ignored and allowed to become weaker if not regularly used.

MULTIPLE INTELLIGENCES

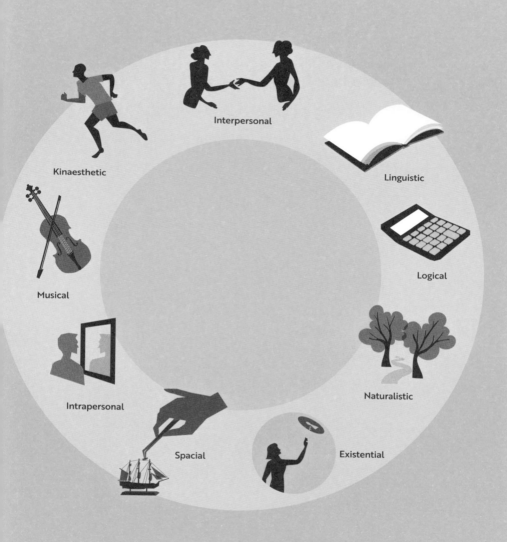

Interpersonal

Kinaesthetic

Linguistic

Musical

Logical

Intrapersonal

Naturalistic

Spacial

Existential

Gardner suggested that we all have varying amounts of the different intelligence types. He suggested that they are located in different brain areas; although it is important to note that this has not been proven. However, it can be helpful for teachers to recognise which intelligence is most dominant in their students. Adapting teaching styles to this can aid learning, especially as typical education systems only focus on verbal linguistic or logical mathematical styles.

Can good leaders get emotional?

→ You wouldn't expect them to get emotional in the boardroom; however, Daniel Goleman's research in 1998 found that what set the best leaders apart was their emotional intelligence. Good leaders need to understand their own and others' emotions.

When one business implemented Goleman's findings and made sure their leaders were high in emotional intelligence, they outperformed their yearly earning goals by 20 per cent. But what is emotional intelligence (EI)? EI is made up of five different skills that allow you to maximise your own and others' performances.

First, self-awareness means having a deep understanding of your own emotions and drives, and knowing how they affect other people. This can show as a thirst for constructive criticism, or in self-deprecating humour. Second, the skill of self-regulation involves control and redirecting impulses, to be able to suspend judgement. Goleman found this creates an environment of trust and fairness. A boss with a fiery temper is not a good leader. Next comes motivation: a good leader must have passion for the job above and beyond money or status. They will often keep score of achievements, which can be contagious in the office environment. Fourth, empathy is an easily recognisable

skill in strong leaders. Managing a team can be like stirring a bubbling cauldron of emotions. A leader needs to understand the emotional make-up of the team members and treat them accordingly. Finally, being able to manage relationships and build networks using social skills is a key component of EI. Goleman describes it as 'friendliness with a purpose'. This sociability is a culmination of the other skills.

The good news is that although the research suggests there is a strong genetic component to EI, it can also be learned. Goleman advises that businesses focus on training the limbic system, as this is the part of the brain that controls our impulses, feelings and drives. Currently, most leadership training instead focusses on the neocortex, which is involved in analytical and technical ability. Even without training, emotional intelligence improves with age: the older we are, the more emotionally mature we tend to be. Although some leaders will still need training, despite their age.

IQ VS EMOTIONAL INTELLIGENCE IN LEADERSHIP

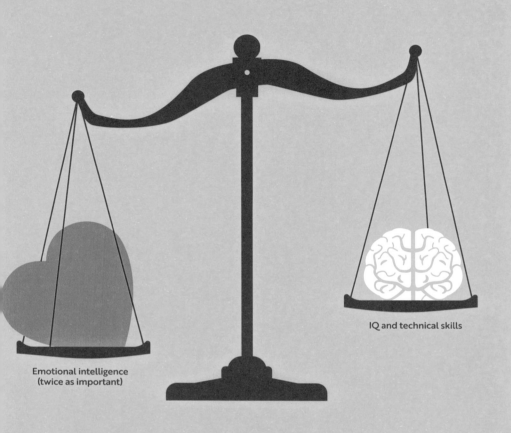

**Emotional intelligence
(twice as important)**

IQ and technical skills

When Goleman and colleagues analysed data from large corporations, they found that intellect was a big driver of outstanding performance in leaders. This was especially true of specific skills, such as having a long-term vision for the business and being adept at big-picture thinking. But above that, emotional intelligence was found to be twice as important as IQ and technical skills in star performers. The higher up the ranks the employee was in the business, the more important emotional intelligence became.

How do you measure personality?

→ Different psychologists have different answers to this question. Freud thought that the secret to personality lies in the unconscious mind and is formed through childhood experiences. Others have used statistical methods to measure personality.

In order to measure personality, psychologists had to try to do a factor analysis on all the data we have from different questionnaires, ratings and scales. The analysis allows us to see hidden patterns and essentially shrink down huge data sets into a smaller number of underlying factors. When McCrae and Costa did this with personality data in 1996, they found five factors emerged that could be used to describe personality. Each trait is measured on its own scale, and together the traits form an acronym OCEAN, or CANOE:

O is for Openness to experience: those people high in it are inventive and curious; those at the lower end tend to be more consistent and cautious.

C is for Conscientiousness: people with lots of this tend to be efficient and organised; those lacking in this trait can be extravagant and careless.

E is for Extraversion: people high in this are easy to spot as they are outgoing and energetic; those lower in this trait are solitary and reserved.

A is for Agreeableness: as you might expect, people high in this are friendly and compassionate; those at the lower end are more critical and rational.

N is for Neuroticism: sometimes called emotional instability, those high in this are sensitive and nervous; people lower in this trait are resilient and confident.

From these traits, McCrae and Costa theorised that all adults can be characterised. Personality is made up of different amounts of the 'Big Five Traits' and how they influence someone's way of thinking, their feelings and their actions. According to this theory, personality traits are basic tendencies that we are born with and that originate from within us. They develop during childhood, and once we reach adulthood, are fully matured and stable. Measuring personality in this way has a number of different uses including predicting some mental and physical health outcomes. The advantage of this theory is that it is much easier to measure than Freud's theory of the unconscious mind. It also considers our internal feelings, unlike the theories that say personality is just the interaction between an individual and their environment.

MEASURING PERSONALITY IN BRAIN STRUCTURE

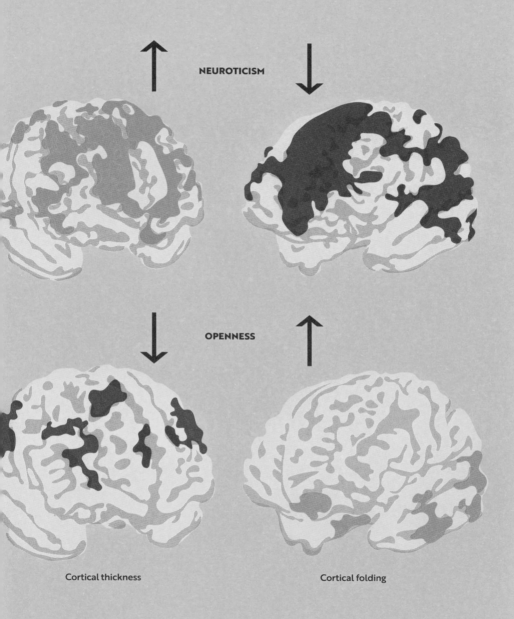

NEUROTICISM

OPENNESS

Cortical thickness

Cortical folding

We might also be able to measure personality traits by looking at our brains. Researchers led by Richelli used brain imaging techniques and found that high levels of neuroticism were associated with thicker areas of the cortex (outer layer of the brain) and fewer folds, whereas openness showed the opposite: less thickness in the cortex and more folds. These differences in brain structure suggest that personality traits probably have a genetic factor to them.

Do we all construct our own worlds?

→ In a sense, yes, we do. In the 1950s, psychologist George Kelly theorised that each of us develops our own constructs that we use to interpret the world. We are like scientists, constantly testing our own hypotheses.

In a given situation, we will have underlying constructs, or mental templates, that help us predict an outcome. They are usually based on our previous experiences. For example, you might have a construct related to greeting people. You might stretch out your hand and predict that they will respond by shaking it, based on what you have seen others do and what you have experienced in the past. If the interaction goes as expected, you know the construct is a useful one to use again. However, if the person goes in for a hug instead, you might need to alter or even abandon the construct.

As we all have different constructs made from our own experiences, we all see the world in our own way, through these predictions. This can also influence the way we remember situations, which can explain why two people might recall the same interaction very differently. Kelly theorised that we pick and choose which constructs to apply when reflecting on events that have multiple interpretations, perhaps to portray our own actions in the best light.

These constructs can be viewed as binary, on a scale between two opposing sides. The side your construct is closest to is called the 'emergent pole' and the other is the 'implicit pole'. For example, one such scale is the adventurous-security scale. If someone has a construct that has adventure as their emergent pole, so they view it as desirable and exciting, they are much more likely to participate in a risky activity such as skydiving than someone who values security and views adventure as high risk, being, as it is, their implicit pole.

Constructs are not fixed. Kelly stated that there are always alternative constructs that might help deal with a situation. He called this constructive alternativism. Although we are all seeing the world through our own constructed lens, it can be important to understand someone else's constructs, to see why they have acted a certain way.

THE EXPERIENCE CYCLE

2
Event

3
Reflection

1
Planning

4
Integration

5
Anticipation

Kelly said the main drivers of the human mind are anticipation and prediction. Every time we experience an event, we anticipate which construct to apply, and evaluate how well it fitted. Afterwards, when reflecting on the outcome, we might consider adjustments to the construct and try to integrate these in anticipation of the next time we experience a similar event. This reoccurrence of the event is important; constructs come from things we experience frequently.

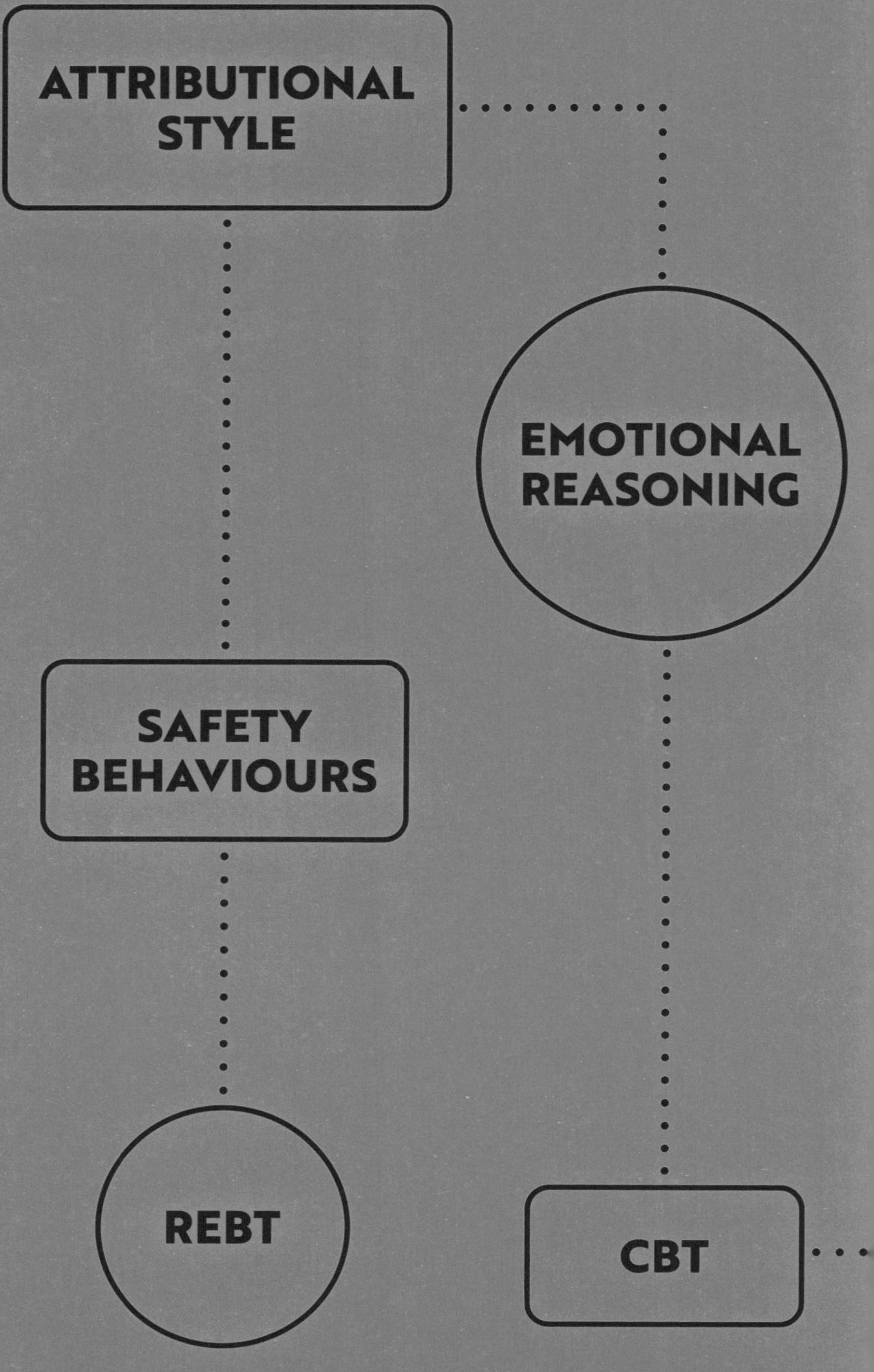
ATTRIBUTIONAL STYLE
EMOTIONAL REASONING
SAFETY BEHAVIOURS
REBT
CBT

TRAUMA

CHAPTER 7

THERAPY

REFLECTIVE
LISTENING

COPING
STRATEGIES

INTRODUCTION

Anyone who has ever felt troubled knows it can be helpful to talk. Over the years, friends, hairdressers and taxicab drivers have been described as therapists, because people feel better after talking to them. But therapy is a lot more than listening and asking a few questions.

Therapy is a treatment for problems such as anxiety or depression, trauma and more extreme difficulties. The earliest records of therapy date back over 3,500 years, when references to 'healing with words' appeared in Egyptian and Greek texts. The Greek philosopher Epictetus noticed that while people may face gritty times, it is the meaning they make of them that matters. This idea that thinking influences feelings is the cornerstone of the most effective therapy today: **COGNITIVE BEHAVIOURAL THERAPY (CBT)**. But it took over a thousand years before studies would confirm the role people's thoughts play in keeping anxiety and depression in place.

Before then, a form of therapy called psychoanalysis was popular. This treatment helped people to discover insights into their personalities and even their dreams. As fascinating as insights are, they rarely lead to change, and this therapy could not be applied with success to serious mental health problems. The field stagnated until the mid-20th century, which suddenly saw a surge of new developments and the foundations of Carl Rogers'

HUMANISTIC THERAPY, a warm-hearted approach based on the healing power of kindness.

Around the same time behaviourism gained traction. This scrutinised animal behaviour to better understand how people learn and unlearn fear. Wolpe developed systematic desensitisation, a form of therapy that helped people to confront rather than avoid their fears. But this approach didn't always change how people thought – someone could still believe that spiders were dangerous yet learn how to be around them.

Stress management arose in the 1960s with Lazarus, who said stress is a marriage between thoughts about an overwhelming situation and capacity to cope. Therapy evolved to bolster coping, with tools such as relaxation. But how well can relaxation banish fear or uplift persistent sadness? Ellis started **RATIONAL EMOTIVE THERAPY**, focussing on the link between how people think and feel.

It was Beck who took this idea to another level, applying science to mental health. He developed and rigorously evaluated psychological models to explain what causes and keeps distress in place. He then targeted problematic thoughts and behaviours in a logical and scientific way, helping people to test their thoughts with experiments and update them with results. Today, CBT is one of the most researched therapies in the world and has the most evidence of effectiveness.

THERAPY MAP

CONGRUENCE
Being our ideal self, which is achieved by developing self-worth through the love and acceptance of others (Rogers).

HUMANISTIC THERAPY
Rogers' therapeutic approach is based on kindness, and the belief that everyone has good inside them and is motivated by trying to reach their potential.

PERSON-CENTRED (OR ROGERIAN) THERAPY
Rogers' therapy approach based on humanistic principles and providing a non-directive, non-judgemental space in which the client is empowered to find their own solutions.

COGNITIVE BEHAVIOURAL THERAPY (CBT)
Encouraging small changes to the way we think and behave daily, through which we can make significant and lasting improvements to how we feel (Beck).

RATIONAL EMOTIVE BEHAVIOUR THERAPY (REBT)
Developed by Albert Ellis, this approach sees client and therapist work to identify irrational beliefs and unhelpful thinking, and replace them with more helpful strategies.

COGNITIVE DISTORTIONS
Unhelpful thinking patterns, such as all-or-nothing thinking and discounting the positive. These can be worked on in therapy, especially CBT.

EMOTIONAL REASONING
Drawing conclusions from a situation or stimulus based on how it makes us feel – an unhelpful thinking pattern, as it doesn't always reflect the reality.

TREATMENT

BEHAVIOURS

BEHAVIOURAL EXPERIMENT
Part of CBT that involves taking practical, controlled steps to change behaviour – perhaps by reducing avoidance – with a therapist if needed, to overcome difficulties.

RICHARD LAZARUS AND SUSAN FOLKMAN
American psychologists (1922–2002 & 1938–) who put forward the notion of stress as an imbalance between demands and resources.

COPING STRATEGIES
Processes that we use to try to manage stress. Problem-based strategies look to remove the problem; emotion-focussed aim to manage the feelings caused by stress.

STRESS BUCKET
Analogy of stressful experiences as water filling up a bucket (our capacity). Coping strategies open the tap to release water (Brabban and Turkington).

KEARNS AND GARDINER'S MOTIVATION FAIRY
Hoping that motivation will magically appear and spur us into action, when in fact getting started with the task generates motivation.

INTRUSIVE NEGATIVE THOUGHTS
Unhelpful thoughts that pop into the mind randomly and unexpectedly. Those who feel bothered or preoccupied by them can develop anxiety issues.

AWARENESS OF THOUGHT PROCESSES
If we become aware of our thought processes, through therapy, for example, we can start to see the bigger picture and be fairer to ourselves.

ATTRIBUTIONAL STYLE
Approach we generally take when assigning a cause to a negative event (Seligman). Those who self-blame are more prone to depression.

THOUGHTS

How can you meet your ideal self?

→ **Perhaps you already have! Or you feel you live in line with your ideal self most of the time. For others, the ideal self can seem miles away, and reaching it requires developing our relationships to build feelings of self-worth.**

The psychologist Carl Rogers used the term incongruence for the state where your current self and your ideal self are far apart. He believed that we all need to feel valued, respected and loved by others, and to be viewed positively by them no matter what. This allows us to develop a sense of self-worth and sets us on the journey towards congruence, moving closer to being our ideal self.

Rogers' approach represents humanistic ideas: that everyone has good inside them and is motivated fundamentally by trying to reach their potential and live a full and satisfying life. This led to a type of counselling called person-centred (or Rogerian) therapy. A key feature of this therapy is that it is non-directive: the therapist provides an open and supportive space but does not direct what should be discussed. The idea is that each of us is the best expert on ourselves, so we are well placed to find solutions for how to reach our goals. The therapist aims to be warm and empathic, fully accepting the client exactly as they are. By supporting the client to understand their own thoughts and feelings as completely as possible, the client has an opportunity to talk through their problems and come to their own conclusions about how to make positive changes.

The idea of a fully functioning ideal self is perhaps just that – more of an idea than something we can actually achieve. It has also been suggested that this concept may not be as relevant in cultures with different values. However, most psychological therapies practised today draw at least partly on Rogers' work. They include the idea of the therapist showing unconditional positive regard towards their client and working to promote a strong therapeutic relationship. The therapeutic relationship (or 'alliance') has been shown to be one of the most important components of treatment that leads to positive outcomes for the client.

REFLECTIVE LISTENING

When was the last time you felt truly listened to? Or fully listened to someone else? Listening is a lot more than just waiting for our turn to speak. Reflective listening is a strategy based on Rogers' work and has two steps: 1) really trying to understand the speaker's point of view, and 2) reflecting this back to them to check you have understood correctly. This is commonly used in therapy to ensure a shared understanding and a strong therapeutic relationship.

Are you coping?

→ It depends how full your bucket is. When our 'stress bucket' overflows, it means the demands placed on us are greater than the resources we feel we have to cope with them. It could be time to ask for help ...

Sadly, a completely stress-free life is a myth. But stress actually serves a purpose: in moderation, it can motivate us and enhance our performance. Too much, however, can be detrimental and cause a range of negative emotions.

The idea of stress as an imbalance between demands and resources was put forward by Richard Lazarus and Susan Folkman. They highlighted that the demands on us might come directly from others but could also be those we perceive, or those we place on ourselves. If we feel that we don't have sufficient personal and social resources to handle those demands, stress is the result. They suggested that the nature of the situation, and the characteristics of the person involved, will affect how they interpret what is happening, and how they cope with it.

Coping is a process that aims to manage stress. Coping strategies can be divided into two types. Problem-based strategies aim to remove the problem, for example, using structured problem solving, time scheduling or obtaining practical help. Emotion-focussed strategies aim to manage the feelings caused by stress. These include strategies such as distraction, meditation, prayer, and talking through your feelings. They also include strategies that may help people manage in the short term, but that can have serious, negative longer-term effects, for example using alcohol or drugs, or avoiding the problem altogether. Problem based coping is often effective because it aims to tackle the cause of the stress. But it can't be used for all problems, and a mixture of both types – excluding the negative strategies – is usually most helpful.

It is probably fair to say that most of the time, the majority of people can cope with the stress they experience. But it is normal and common to have times when we feel we aren't coping. If this happens, the best thing you can do is to talk to someone about it, perhaps a friend, family member or health professional. You don't have to struggle alone.

THE STRESS BUCKET

Brabban and Turkington's stress bucket is a simple way to think about our capacity for managing stress and how to prevent an 'overflow' of feeling that can be detrimental to our well-being. Stressful experiences are the water that starts to fill up the bucket. Coping and 'destressing' strategies open the tap to release water. By monitoring our water level and keeping the tap open, we can keep stress under control.

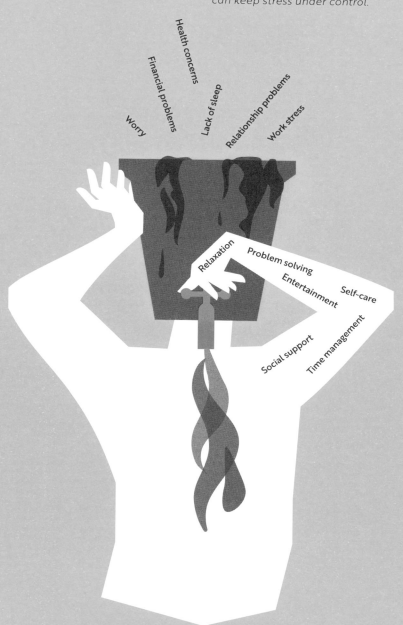

Where do negative thoughts come from?

→ Some come from being stressed, low or run down. Some may be our brain taking a short cut by using our past experiences as a guide. Others may be purely random. Whatever the cause, it doesn't make them true.

It is likely that there is no single cause for the negative thoughts we experience. Some appear to pop into the mind randomly and unexpectedly. Studies have shown that this type of intrusive negative thought is actually very common. They are often about things we might consider to be inappropriate, blasphemous or harmful. Although many people may be able to dismiss them as having little meaning, others may feel more bothered by these thoughts and become preoccupied by them. This process has been linked to anxiety problems such as obsessive-compulsive disorder.

Feeling anxious or low is also enough to generate more frequent negative thoughts. We may find ourselves dwelling on past mistakes, criticising ourselves or worrying about the future. Martin Seligman suggested the idea that our minds get trained into a certain way of thinking based on our early experiences. If we've had a number of difficult experiences in earlier life we might end up expecting things will go badly, and that it will be our fault when they do. This is referred to as an attributional style – the approach we generally take when attributing a cause to a negative event. Some people have a style that generally assumes that stressful or difficult events happen because they have done something wrong, and that this is unlikely to change and will affect many areas of their life. This style is thought to increase the risk of depression, because we may end up feeling helpless, as though we have no control over the situation.

Crucially, just because we have a negative thought, it doesn't mean it is true: thoughts are not facts. And our styles of thinking are not set in stone. By learning to become more aware of our thought processes, we can start to spot when we might be missing the bigger picture or being unfair on ourselves, and therefore choose to take a different approach. This is a core idea behind a number of psychological therapies.

THOUGHT SUPPRESSION

Take a look at this giant, fluffy, red rabbit. Now close your eyes for 30 seconds and make sure you don't think about the rabbit. Try as hard as you can not to think about it. Studies generally show that the harder people try to avoid thinking about something, the more likely it is to come to mind. Trying to suppress negative thoughts might actually cause them to happen more often. Many clients in therapy find discovering this very helpful.

Why are we irrational?

→ Probably because we're not robots. Humans are incapable of operating on a purely rational level because we have emotions that guide how we make decisions and how we behave.

Often, having our emotions guide us can be helpful. People sometimes describe having a 'gut feeling' about something, or 'following their heart' when making a decision. The influence of emotions can help us focus on the things that matter most to us, while avoiding unpleasant or dangerous situations. But sometimes, being strongly guided by emotions can lead us into unhelpful patterns of thinking and behaviour, which can reinforce feelings of anxiety and depression. For example, if someone feels anxious in a crowded place, they may have the belief that 'because I feel nervous, then the situation must be dangerous'. They may then decide to go home and try to avoid crowds in future, which might result in them feeling lonelier and more held back by the anxiety.

The idea that we can get stuck in unhelpful thinking is the focus of a range of therapies, including rational emotive behaviour therapy (REBT), developed by Albert Ellis. In this therapy, the client and therapist work to identify beliefs that might be considered irrational, and other patterns of unhelpful thinking, so the beliefs can be challenged and replaced with more helpful strategies. In the example above, the crowded situation led to a belief that the person was in danger. In reality, there weren't any signs that the situation was dangerous, but the person came to this conclusion based on the anxiety they felt. This is an example of unhelpful thinking called emotional reasoning.

Other unhelpful thinking patterns, or cognitive distortions, include all-or-nothing thinking, where we view things as black or white – for example, 'If I don't do this perfectly, then it's a complete failure.' Another is discounting the positive, where we find reasons to minimise or dismiss positive experiences, and instead tend to dwell on or magnify the negatives. By discussing these in therapy, the client may feel more able to identify when these happen and choose to respond to those situations in a different way.

FACING FEAR

Phobias of specific objects or situations, such as spiders, blood or flying, are some of the most common mental health difficulties. Many know that their fears are irrational, but this doesn't stop the strong feelings when faced with the phobic object. Phobias have both genetic and environmental causes, and are maintained by the way we think and behave. Fortunately, phobias generally respond well to psychological therapy, and significant progress can be achieved in as little as a single therapy session.

Will changing your behaviour change your mind?

→ Our thoughts, emotions and behaviours are all connected. Doing things differently can influence what we think and feel, and the power of this can benefit all of us.

Many of us will have had the experience of putting off doing something, such as exercising or starting a new project. We simply lack the motivation, and as this continues day after day, we can end up feeling guilty, low in mood and self-critical. Hugh Kearns and Maria Gardiner (2011) refer to this as 'waiting for the motivation fairy' – hoping that one day the motivation will magically appear and spur us into action. But the fairy doesn't exist, and research shows it is actually the other way round – getting started with the task generates motivation to keep going and do more. Changing our behaviour to start something, even if we don't feel like it initially, can ultimately have a positive effect on our mood and our thinking.

This link between thoughts, feelings and behaviours is central to cognitive behavioural therapy (CBT), first developed by Aaron Beck. By making small changes to the way we think and behave on a regular basis, we can make significant and lasting improvements to how we feel. In some CBT sessions, the client works together with their therapist to experiment with changing their behaviours in order to challenge the negative beliefs that are keeping them feeling low or anxious. For example, someone with post-traumatic stress disorder following a train crash may believe strongly that if they use the train now, another accident will happen and they will be badly injured or die. As a result, they avoid all public transport, which means they cannot work or see friends. A behavioural experiment for this client might involve taking the brave step of doing things differently to reduce this avoidance – perhaps taking the train together with their therapist to the next station. By changing their behaviour like this, they can discover first-hand that their feared predictions are less likely than they thought. This also helps them make significant progress towards overcoming their difficulties

SAFETY BEHAVIOURS

People with social anxiety often feel stared at by others. To try and prevent this happening, people generally keep their head down and avoid eye contact. These strategies are called safety behaviours, because people use them to feel safer in fearful situations. But surprisingly, safety behaviours generally make anxiety worse. By enrolling in CBT, people discover a powerful truth: that others aren't particularly focussed on them, and that this feeling is an illusion caused by the anxiety.

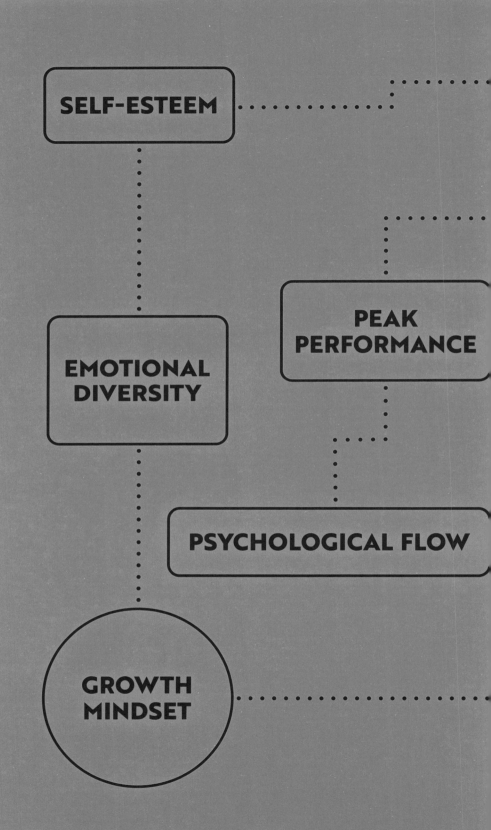

CHAPTER 8

POSITIVE PSYCHOLOGY

- PERSONALITY TRAITS
- HAPPINESS
- REWARDS

INTRODUCTION

A lot of us think that winning the lottery would instantly make us happy. But happiness has little to do with a heaving bank balance. This chapter covers some of the core ingredients for happy living that psychology has pinpointed over the years, why they're important and how to get them.

First, we need robust **SELF-ESTEEM**. This means we need to hold positive opinions about ourselves. Since opinions are thoughts, not facts, the good news is that it's possible to improve our self-esteem by changing the way we think. Cultivating healthy attitudes can help enormously with this, such as seeing excitement in new challenges, and believing both that we can be successful and that we are as deserving as others.

People with great self-esteem tend to be more successful in what they put their mind to, and are even healthier, whereas those people – especially teenagers – who struggle to think positively about themselves are more likely to develop problems. The **SELF-SERVING BIAS** can help foster and protect our esteem. It means attributing successes to ourselves and bad outcomes to others or the world. Psychologists say it takes a while to get comfortable in our own skin, with self-esteem seeming to settle in our sixties, when we have the wisdom and skill to nurture the habit of healthy thinking.

The second key ingredient to ensure happy living is **EMOTIONAL DIVERSITY,** making sure we go out of our way to create opportunities to feel a range of upbeat emotions. **A GROWTH MINDSET** is important too. It's about believing that effort and practice are as important as natural-born talent, and seizing rather than avoiding new challenges. Parents can support a growth mindset for their children by rewarding effort instead of praising ability. The perks of a growth mindset are that it can protect us when times are tough and can be developed through training. Studies of low-income families found that children with this mindset were more likely to achieve than those who shared similar levels of hardship but not the same mindset.

People are happier when they are absorbed in the task at hand, whatever that task is, from answering emails to washing dishes, a famous finding linked to psychologist **MIHALY CSIKSZENTMIHALYI**. They're even happier when they're engaged in tasks that are challenging enough to be stimulating but not so challenging that they're overwhelming. Absorbing our attention in the task at hand stops the mind wandering and helps rewarding feelings to flow.

All of the ingredients that keep happy feelings in place are also key to surviving and thriving, or what psychologists more commonly call flourishing. We're more likely to flourish if we train ourselves to be happy.

POSITIVE PSYCHOLOGY MAP

COOPERSMITH SELF-ESTEEM INVENTORY
Questionnaire developed to assess children's esteem in the context of peers, parents, school and self, by looking for simple behavioural and cognitive signs of self-esteem.

SELIGMAN'S PERMA™ THEORY
Set of five evidence-based building blocks to promote flourishing: positive emotion, engagement, relationships, meaning and purpose.

POSITIVE PSYCHOLOGY
Focusses on positive, valued experiences and concepts, such as a growth mindset, training a happy mind, flourishing, self-esteem and emotional diversity.

SELF-ESTEEM
The opinion we hold of ourselves, which can be improved by changing the way we think. Protected by the self-serving bias.

SELF-SERVING BIAS
Attributing successes to ourselves and bad outcomes to others or the world, thereby protecting self-esteem.

HEALTHSPAN
Time spent living well, in good health and free from disease. A concept that has derived from our extended lifespan and increased quality of life.

FIXED MINDSET
An inflexible way of thinking; sticking to what we are good at and veering away from new challenges.

EMOTIONAL DIVERSITY
Experiencing an abundance of positive emotions that are the key to well-being, reduced stress and better health.

FLOURISHING

PHYSIOLOGICAL MARKERS
Measurable changes in the body, such as blood pressure, depth of breath, heart rate variability and activation in certain muscle groups.

PSYCHOLOGICAL FLOW
Universal human capability that requires positivity and sustained, seemingly effortless attention, and which is key to a life worth living (Csikszentmihalyi).

PEAK PERFORMANCE
When optimum behaviours combine to produce an exceptional or best performance.

ARGYLE'S COMPONENTS OF HAPPINESS
Three key factors of happiness, with cognitive and emotional aspects include: satisfaction with life, the presence of positive affect and the absence of negative affect.

MIHALY CSIKSZENTMIHALYI
Hungarian-American psychologist (1934–2021) who travelled the world investigating happiness and creativity, and who coined the term 'psychological flow'.

PERSONALITY TRAITS
Character attributes that distinguish a person. They are typically positive or negative and stable over time, meaning they are hard to change.

GROWTH MINDSET
Being open to change and new opportunities; embracing challenges; learning from failure; believing in effort and practice.

FLOW

Are you worth it?

→ **You might answer this by considering how much you like yourself. If you feel as deserving as other people, believe you have 'what it takes' and are happy enough to step past your comfort zone, then you're brimming with self-esteem.**

Who comes to mind when you think about someone strong in self-esteem? Are they super-human or have they honed how to think positively about themselves? Self-esteem is the opinion we hold of ourselves. As opinions are thoughts not facts, this means we can change our self-esteem by changing how we think. Some indicators of healthy self-esteem include how confident we feel in expressing our opinion, our willingness to try new things, our belief that we'll be successful and our sense that we're at least as deserving as other people.

Research in this field was sparked in the late 1960s in American schools. Educators and researchers realised the benefits of positive self-esteem as an outcome of schooling, rather than focussing only on academic achievement. The Coopersmith Self-esteem Inventory was developed to assess children's esteem in the context of peers, parents, school and self; with questionnaires tapping simple behavioural and cognitive signs of self-esteem.

More recently, large studies beginning at birth and following through to adulthood suggest that drops in self-esteem during adolescence can lead to poor physical health, mental ill health, criminal behaviours and worse financial prospects. Poor self-esteem can spark a vicious cycle of unfortunate experiences, gradually worsening outcomes and distress.

Thankfully, we have cognitive biases that serve to keep self-esteem healthy and in check. The self-serving bias means that people are most likely to attribute successes and good things to themselves, and failures and bad outcomes to others or the world. If something turns out well, you tell yourself you did it; if it went badly, you look to other explanations. The good news is that self-esteem, once adolescence has passed, can improve continually as you gather positive life experiences all the way up to your sixties where it stabilises and only begins to drop again in your nineties.

MEASURING SELF-ESTEEM

We measure self-esteem by asking
questions. We might ask a child how well
they think they do at school, whether they
believe that they make friends easily or how
much their parents seem to value them.
In adulthood, this progresses to questions
about how much pride people might take in
their work and other achievements, as well
as questions about friends and family.

Is there a short cut to happiness?

→ In the short term, you can try sticking a pencil between your teeth, but in the longer term, other strategies fare better. Psychological science has a lot to say about how best to kick-start and sustain happy feelings.

If you are looking for a short cut to happiness, or at least a place to start, there is something you can try right away. All you need is a pen or pencil. Studies have shown that sticking a pencil between your teeth activates the same muscles as a smile, making you feel happier and more light-hearted. But this effect seems to vanish when you remove the pencil, and might only work if you were happy to start with. If you are looking for something longer lasting, you need to consider the key ingredients that encourage happiness.

Michael Argyle recognised the importance of happiness, or 'subjective well-being' (from research in the 1980s), when studies of depression outnumbered those on happiness 17:1. The components of happiness, according to Argyle, involve separate cognitive and emotional aspects. The three key factors include satisfaction with life (social, work and leisure), the presence of positive affect and the absence of negative affect.

We know that beyond a certain level of security, money does not make us happy. We also know that we get happier as we age. But what can we change to short-cut our route to happiness? Studies in neuroscience give clues and suggest that the key formula for happy living involves meeting or exceeding our own expectations. It's not how well something might be going for us, but whether or not it is better than we expected.

More recent research tells us that instead of focussing all of our attention on happiness, the key to well-being is to seek out day-to-day emotional diversity. Experiencing an abundance of positive emotions, such as interest, calm, pride, gratitude or inspiration, reduces stress and inflammation, leading to better health and, therefore, more reasons to smile. So, although there may not be a steadfast short cut, there certainly are many routes to happiness.

DIVERSITY OF POSITIVE EMOTIONS

Sticking a pencil between your teeth might spark a smile and provide a short cut to happiness. But for longer-lasting results, seek out activities that inspire a range of upbeat feelings, such as learning a new recipe or solving a problem with the help of colleagues. We're happier when we're being creative and connecting with other people.

Will changing your mindset change your mind?

→ Yes! Shifting from a fixed mindset to a growth mindset will not only transform the way you think, it will supercharge your success, performance and power to bounce back after failure.

Shifting from a fixed mindset to a growth mindset powers success in business, parenting and school. Carol Dweck suggests that changing your mindset means challenging your underlying beliefs about learning and intelligence.

How would you feel if you were asked to learn an entirely new skill, something you knew would stretch you well beyond your comfort zone? Instead of saying, 'I can't. I'll stick to what I'm good at,' people who say, 'I can't do that yet,' then embrace the challenge tend to show more resilience in the face of failure. They learn from errors instead of quitting – and they achieve more as a result. Someone with a growth mindset believes that effort and practice is worth at least as much as, if not more than, natural-born ability.

The idea of the growth mindset is important for positive psychology because it challenges the idea that intelligence, education and income are crucial for success. For example, a study looking at a large number of families in Chile found that children from lower-income homes were less likely to have a growth mindset. However, for those who did, it acted as a buffer against the negative impact of low income on achievement. The growth mindset, therefore, can be a real protective factor in difficult circumstances.

Crucially, the growth mindset can be trained. Studies show that teaching children to expect their abilities to improve and their brain to develop, as well as nudging oneself beyond what's comfortable, are key to graceful growth. Compared to children who believe their abilities are set in stone, children trained to adopt a growth mindset show boosts in motivation and grades. Rewarding effort instead of praising ability creates confidence and persistence. Adopting this mindset in the face of a difficult environment, a challenge or a failure means focussing on how to move forward, how to face more challenges and how to continue learning.

THE GROWTH MINDSET

Changing your mindset influences your beliefs, effort, approach to challenges and response to failure. Encouraging a growth mindset allows people to focus on the future, embracing new challenges to fulfil their potential.

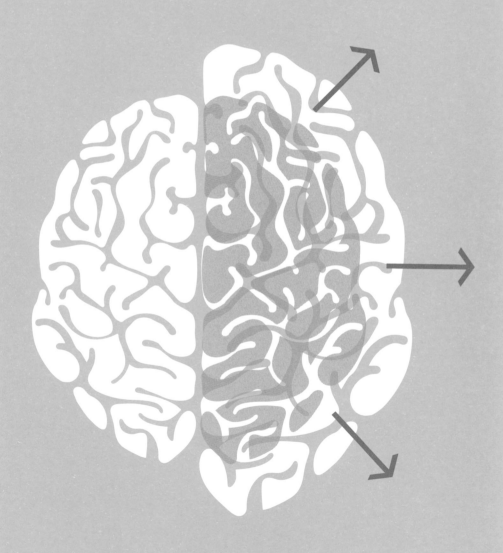

Can psychology help you flourish?

⟶ **Living a good life is about more than surviving: it means thriving. Psychology shows us how to tap our full potential; how to transform an ordinary life into an extraordinary one.**

We all know that stress, mental ill health, social inequality and trauma are detrimental to well-being. But did you know they are costly when it comes to longevity and lifespan? Since medical advances have added years to our lifespan, the field has expanded its focus to include healthspan – time spent living well. How do we ensure quality for the extra quantity of years we'll likely have? How do we live our lives well?

Psychological research tells us heaps about how to live an extraordinary life. Rather than spotlighting how to eliminate or overcome suffering and distress, new research shines light on how we can flourish. Flourishing is about tapping our full potential, about transforming an ordinary life to an extraordinary one. It means living our lives with purpose.

Martin Seligman's developments in the field of positive psychology have included a set of evidence-based building blocks to promote something called flourishing.

PERMA™ theory builds on Maslow's hierarchy of needs. Only once the building blocks to a good life have been managed (safety, shelter, food, water) can the high-level factors (esteem, cognitive and aesthetic needs, self-actualisation) become the focus of an individual or a community. The five factors that seem to contribute to flourishing are level of positive emotion, engagement, relationships, meaning and purpose, and accomplishment.

We know that the things we measure affect the things we do. If we focus purely on classic indicators of success, such as the money we make or the number of things we own as an individual, or just on the grades of school children or productivity on a political and economic level, PERMA™ theory suggests that we miss critical components of flourishing. Just as medical researchers need to be concerned not only with the number of years we live, psychological researchers need to be concerned with increasing the number of years spent flourishing.

THE BUILDING BLOCKS TO FLOURISHING

Meaning

Accomplishments

Relationships

Engagement

For humans to flourish, we first need to feed our basic needs for security, shelter and nutrition. Then we can focus on leading lives aligned with our values and sense of purpose. Valuing relationships, creating opportunities to feel upbeat and finding meaning in what we do are some of the core steps to flourishing.

Positive emotion

Should we all just go with the flow?

⟶ If you want to peak your well-being and performance, the answer is yes! Psychologist Mihaly Csikszentmihalyi said that psychological flow requires positivity and sustained attention, and could be the key to a life worth living.

When was the last time that you were totally absorbed with the task at hand? A time when you were stretched to your skill limit, performed at your peak and felt your best? Mihaly Csikszentmihalyi travelled around the world asking people just that. Exploring this experience for musicians, surgeons, dancers, farmers, sheep herders and factory workers led him to conclude that psychological flow is a universal human capability that is key to a life worth living. Flow state incorporates a feeling of effortless attention and positive emotion.

What happens in the mind and body when a classical pianist performs at their best? Studies have found measurable physiological markers during flow. These markers include changes in blood pressure, depth of breath, heart rate variability and activation in the muscle group recruited for smiling. While flow indicates the mental state required, peak performance describes the optimum behaviours.

The skilled classical pianist will feel alert but calm, confident but challenged, and totally absorbed in the present moment, and they will produce an exceptional piece of music as a result. Although we may be tempted to strive to achieve flow for boosts to productivity, studies show that the experience itself is rewarding. The committed effort to achieve the flow state leads to contentment and happiness.

Flow and peak performance are not just associated with making music. People report achieving flow through sport, work, creative hobbies, games, music, religion or spirituality and learning. Conscientious individuals tend to experience more flow, but certain personality traits can block flow, with bad moods keeping it at bay. We're most likely to flow when we're absorbed in tasks that are challenging enough to be stimulating but not so challenging that they're overwhelming. While there may be plenty of barriers to flow that prevent people from getting into 'the zone', it is clearly a state worth pursuing.

PEAK PERFORMANCE AND FLOW

Mental flow is about being fully absorbed in the task at hand. It's a blend of fortified focus, upbeat feelings and a complete lack of self-consciousness. A classical pianist giving the performance of a lifetime will experience flow at the peak of their performance. Entering flow, or 'the zone', is like letting go as you're swept along by a river, relaxing into the journey rather than stressing about the destination.

FURTHER EXPLORATION

BOOKS

Beck, A.T., et al. *Cognitive Therapy of Depression*. New York: Guilford Press, 1979

Bond, M. *Wayfinding: The Art and Science of How We Find and Lose Our Way*. London: Picador, 2020

Corsini, R. & Wedding, D. *Current Psychotherapies*. Totnes: Brooks/Cole Publishing Company, 2018

Deutsch Lezak, M., et al. *Neuropsychological Assessment*. Oxford: Oxford University Press, 2012

Dunn, J. *The Beginnings of Social Understanding*. Cambridge, MA: Harvard University Press, 1988

Erikson, E. *Identity, Youth, and Crisis*. New York: W. W. Norton, 1968

Erikson, E.H. *Childhood and Society*. New York: W. W. Norton & Company, 1993

Morrison, A.P. (ed.). *A Casebook of Cognitive Therapy for Psychosis*. New York: Brunner-Routledge, 2002

Seth, A. *Being You*. London: Faber & Faber, 2021

Slater, A. & Bremner, J. *An introduction to Developmental Psychology*. London: BPS Blackwell. Third ed., 2017

Wild, J. *Be Extraordinary: 7 Key Skills to Transform Your Life From Ordinary to Extraordinary*. Boston: Little, Brown Book Group, 2020

JOURNALS

Borke, H. (1975). Piaget's mountains revisited. *Developmental Psychology*, 11(2), 240–243

Bruner, J. (1981). The social context of language acquisition. *Language & Communication*, 1(2), 155–178

Dunn, J. (1994). Understanding others and the social world: Current issues in developmental research and their relation to preschool experiences and practice. *Journal of Applied Developmental Psychology*, 15(4), 571–583

Flavell, J.H. (1996). Piaget's legacy. *Psychological Science, 7*(4), 200–203

Kearns, H. & Gardiner, M. (2011). Waiting for the motivation fairy. *Nature*, 472, 127

Nader, K., Schafe, G.E. & LeDoux, J.E. (2000a). The labile nature of consolidation theory. *Nature Reviews Neuroscience*. 1, 216–219

Wegner, D.M., et al. (1987). Paradoxical effects of thought suppression. *Journal of Personality and Social Psychology, 53*(1), 5–13

ONLINE RESOURCES

www.simplypsychology.org

www.nationalelfservice.net

Every Mind Matters
www.nhs.uk/every-mind-matters

Mind www.mind.org.uk

NOTES ON CONTRIBUTORS

CONSULTANT EDITOR

Dr Jennifer Wild

Jennifer Wild is Professor of Military Mental Health at the University of Melbourne. She holds an affiliate position at the University of Oxford, where she developed evidence-based interventions to prevent PTSD for emergency responders, now being delivered internationally. She is an author who has also written for *Nature News*, the BBC, *The Times*, *The Sunday Times* and *The Psychologist*. Professor Wild applies science to understanding and preventing mental ill health.

ILLUSTRATOR

Robert Brandt

Based in the UK, for over twenty years Robert Brandt has been a visual communicator with a focus on illustrating technical and scientific subjects ranging from astrophysics to biochemistry. He works with experts to make complex topics accessible to a wide audience in publishing, industry and education.

CONTRIBUTORS

Michael Bond

Michael Bond is a writer specialising in human psychology and behaviour. He was previously a senior editor at *New Scientist*.

Sophie Grant

Sophie Grant is a research assistant at the Oxford Centre for Anxiety Disorders and Trauma (OxCADAT) working on the dissemination of internet-based cognitive therapy, for social anxiety disorder and post-traumatic stress disorder, into the NHS.

Aimee McKinnon

Aimee McKinnon is a clinical psychologist and researcher. Her clinical and research interests include prevention and early intervention, risk, PTSD, and complex PTSD.

Helen Pilcher

Helen Pilcher has a PhD in cell biology from London's Institute of Psychiatry, as well as degrees in psychology and neuroscience. She used to work as a reporter for *Nature*, and managed the Royal Society's Science in Society Program. She now writes and talks about science. She has penned many popular science books, as well as news and features for the likes of *The Guardian*, *New Scientist* and *Science Focus*.

Dr Graham Thew

Dr Graham Thew is a clinical psychologist and researcher at the University of Oxford and Oxford Health NHS Foundation Trust. He provides evidence-based psychological therapies for adults with anxiety or depression, and researches how digital technology can enhance therapy to help people get the most out of their treatment.

Gabriella Tyson

Gabriella Tyson is a PhD candidate at the University of Oxford, whose research focusses on preventing mental health problems in at-risk populations.

Trinity de Simone

Trinity de Simone is a graduate research assistant at OxCADAT. The team specialise in the research and treatment of anxiety and stress disorders.

Abbie Wilkins

Abbie Wilkins is an associate lecturer of psychological therapies at the University of Exeter and specialises in complex PTSD at OxCADAT.

INDEX

ACKNOWLEDGEMENTS

I'd like to express my enormous gratitude
to our commissioning editor, Kate Duffy, for
the right mix of perseverance, guidance and
patience to see this project through to a
timely fruition. I'd like to thank Katie Crous
for her exquisite copy editing and attention
to detail. Huge thanks to all of the co-authors
for sharing enlivened psychological insights
and making this book possible. I'd like to
thank my sister, Allison Wild, for her breadth
of expertise and for being available to bounce
ideas back and forth. Thanks to Mark Todd
and Amy Sedgwick for spirited chats and
kindness. Finally, big thanks to my writing
companions, Sami, Zak and Pip.

Jennifer Wild

UniPress Books would like to thank Robert
Brandt for his illuminating illustrations and
Luke Herriott for his elegant design work.